FROM BEiNG TO BEiNG

유에서유

From Being to Being

by Oh Eun

Translated by Shyun J. Ahn

Black Ocean
Boston - Chicago

유에서 유
Oh Eun © 2016
Originally published in 2016 by Moonji Publishing Co., Ltd.

Black Ocean
P.O. Box 52030
Boston, MA 02205
blackocean.org

Cover Art and Design by Abby Haddican | abbyhaddican.com
Book Design by Taylor D. Waring | taylordwaring.com

ISBN: 978-1-965154-05-2
Library of Congress Control Number: 2025931730

This book is published with the support of the Literature Translation Institute of Korea (LTI Korea).

FIRST EDITION
Printed in Canada

CONTENTS

Part III

Part IV

Commentary

Do you know why honey tastes so sweet?
'Cause its taste has been neither dreamed nor dreaming;
'Cause it's a future; 'Cause it hasn't arrived.

In my pocket, I carried many sweet words born out of my ignorance.
—Oh Eun, Summer 2016

TRANSLATOR'S NOTE

One day in the 2010s, I picked up Oh Eun's *Yu Eseo Yu* at a bookstore. Back in my room, I underscored lines in "Guwon" (Salvation) with a pencil. I thought, "I would love to translate this book, but someone must be working on this awesome book already, right?" Fast forward to the summer of 2020 when I met Jake Levine, the Moon Country series editor at Black Ocean for the first time. While drinking at a microbrewery next to Kim Gwang-seok Street, Jake suggested that I translate a poetry collection for Black Ocean. As much as I was honored, I wanted to focus on research, so I did not accept the suggestion on the spot. Two and a half years later I emailed Jake to see if he was still interested in me doing a book. I asked Jake what book they would be interested in publishing and that I had no particular preference. Jake responded, "Do you know Oh Eun? I would love to do a book by Oh Eun. And I don't think anyone is working on his books right now." Surprised no one was working on this book, I accepted his recommendation right away and started to work on Oh Eun's *Yu Eseo Yu*, turning it into the English translation, *From Being to Being*.

Though I was exhilarated by this fateful opportunity, I was apprehensive at the same time. Oh's poems push readers to experience the Korean language beyond its ordinary use. However, due to the linguistic difference between English and Korean, there is so much a translator can do to reanimate this experience. Despite this inherent challenge, I strived to come up with the best translations by contemplating the meaning of each line, the poet's intention, and what

I imagined to be the readers' reception. In doing so, I often had to select and emphasize one component of language over others. For instance, the second line in "A book that sells well / A book that wells sell" ("A Book") deviates from the semantic meaning of the original text. A literal translation would read "A book that cuts arms." I made this choice because it was clear that Oh intended to play with the sounds *pal* and *jal*, rather than communicating a sensical message. Conversely, I occasionally prioritized meaning over wordplay. In his epigraph, Oh plays with honey (*ggul*) and the future tense of "to dream" (*gguda*), as they are homonymous. However, this pun cannot be revived in English without drastically changing the meaning of the text, so I decided to let it go. In addition, I sporadically added a pun or rhyme that Oh did not write to capture his playfulness. Another challenge was the transition between tenses. In English, shifting from past to present tense can feel much more dramatic than in Korean. When this occurred, I diverged from the original text to choose what feels natural for English readers. I hope my deliberate choices will help English readers enjoy Oh Eun's *From Being to Being* as much as possible.

Before I end this note, I want to thank Oh Eun, Jake Levine, and Black Ocean for entrusting this invaluable work to me. It was an immense delight to jump into this cheerful play, and I am deeply grateful.

January 2024
Shyun (Suhyun) J. Ahn

Part I
I Saw a Feather

THE FEELING OF A SEASON

I liked a corner
When I leaned on it
I became a waiting person

Winter blew in and backed out
I felt something disappear
so I fumbled in my pocket

A dog was coming to me
A dog I had never seen before
The dog must have felt the same

I brushed past the dog
The dog checked me out

Growing used to our faces
Growing used to our scents

Autumn was not yet mature but
something had ripened in my heart
so I looked back unwittingly

The dog was sweating but
it kept its skin on
Nothing could be done

I was sweating but
I kept my coat on
Nothing had been done

We are still in our husks

I felt something in my hand
so I put my hand in my pocket

When I opened a crumpled receipt
it was fortunately summer

People whose feelings linger
live a little longer
in one season more than others

DIZZYING

My favorite word vanished in my dream. I forgot the word when I woke up. In the mirror, I looked speechless.

Somedays we listen to the same song in different spaces at the same time in different moods. We arrive later than the last station. The meeting doesn't convene. Only the melody flows.

I spilled everything I was carrying. Solids flowed like liquids. The fonts attached to a book leaf scamper away, putting on punctuation marks. My favorite word evaporated.

Pour water on the impossible. It'll be possible. It'll be usable. Set fire to the possible. It'll be impossible. It'll be magnificent. No one will lay a finger on it.

I read a diary from ten years ago today. The weather was clear. It rains ten years later today. It finally rains today. I intently observe the eraser marks. Some words are not chosen at last, not loved at length. Only their traces remain.

Somedays we listen to different songs in the same space at different times in the same mood. We depart earlier than the first station. The impossible becomes possible. A delusion becomes magnificent.

The moment a dying person contemplates dinner, a restaurant closes its doors. Menus are grimacing. My stomach is churning. I'm being strangled. Right now, right now.

Time and space are clumped in a single word.

AN OLD TALE

Here is an old tale. A tale that couldn't be shared in the olden days. A tale that can finally be shared today. The very tale that made hands fly in from everywhere, covering the mouths of those about to share it.

A tale everyone knows but its end remains unknown. A tale where those trying to reach the end were brought to the end midway. A tale that is never-ending to the end. A tale that repeats.

A tale passed discreetly by word of mouth. A tale that mystifies more with each passing day. A tale that started to spread faintly only after so-and-so died. A tale that is growing suspicious.

A tale that will be alive tomorrow and the day after, whether you are here or not. A tale destined to be alone no matter what. A tale that is as distant as the olden days, as vague as the future, yet continues today. A tale that comes to life ever more vividly in the underground and the air.

Here is an old tale. It is still here. It is still here, pristine. A tale of us living here in this moment. A tale that we cannot spell out even if we open our mouths. A tale that lacks a clear answer even if we lend our ears. A tale that is much the same.

BLANK

Don't cut your nails at night
A ghost will haunt you

A gust rushes if stars flicker at night
All enticing things are dangerous

Everything turns frosty if the night sky is especially clear
Keep your head up and walk upright

All my grandmother's secrets nested in the night

Don't traverse the dark road alone at night
Always watch your back

A day fades
A night approaches

The day was a series of misfires

I couldn't mask my expression
The night was loaded
I sensed it closing in

All around
silent blanks
exploded like firecrackers

Speak softly at night
A rat can do anything if it hears you

Secrets, roaring,
scrambled to fill the empty spots in my pillow

JAMAIS VU

How can that be?
A person clings and wails

Here it can be
A person answers impassively

The moment the impossible became possible,

My body crumbled
My heart crumbled
With a thump
a world crumbled

Though I've never left here
I've never felt I belonged

As though it was my first time, I was as clumsy as ever

People surround people
Some surround and some are surrounded
No one says a word

People find people awkward
People are people yet awkward as people

The person who cried here
barely walks clinging to the road
Their home should be somewhere near

Homeward bound a person meets a person
A familiar smell is wafting
Good day
some words can be said on not-so-good days

To feel an ache inside
is to look fine on the outside
I thought I barely became myself through winter
yet spring stood frozen

A person stands on the sinking ground
A person who does not belong here
is here

How can there be such a person?

They are here
Probably here

TODAY'S VALUE OF FEELING

I saw a feather
The moment my heart was lightening up,
the feather was falling to the ground
My eyes blinked on their own

Something soared in the distance
It was dazzling

It's fine to say the sun is burning
It's fine to say the sun is scorching
I gathered sunlight with all my body

It's fine to say the wind is cozy
It's fine to say the wind is soft
I drew air into all my heart

Today's worth of energy surged
Today's worth of feeling surged

To have a surge
To acquire what I don't have
To hold on to another thing for a while

I can't see inside my body
Even when I'm not walking
I just know they are moving

I saw a feather
I saw a quivering feather

When I come back to my room
it's burning and cozy
it's scorching and soft
I saw time
composed of today's value of memory

The scenery that emerges just before falling asleep
sluggishly
appears in my dream

A soaring feather appears in my dream
Tossing and turning under the blanket
I finally comprehend tomorrow's value of feeling

DO YOU KNOW SO-AND-SO?

I want to know someone
so I asked people I knew

The dude who's fat?
The dude who writes a poem?
The dude who only reads philosophy books?
The dude who stammers when he's nervous?
The dude who dated so-and-so?
The dude who was dumped by another so-and-so?

Words about so-and-so burst carelessly
As if so-and-so is any so-so dog
they devoured him and ripped him apart like butchers
Mean laughter filled the gaping wound
As they eagerly sprayed saliva on each other's grinning faces
no-matter-what converged with by-all-means

Tarnished coins spilled from a pocket
The Dabo Pagoda collapsed
The ears of rice scattered
Admiral Yi Sun-sin lay prone
A crane plummeted

I wished not to know the person I sought to know
The person I knew felt like a person I had never known

You can know the back of a coin without seeing it

I didn't want to be so-and-so
so I cloaked my face and wandered aimlessly

A HOLE

I urge a hole. Until the light
is pierced
no one asked
what lies beyond
Like the dead of night
we were forbearing and intimate
In broad daylight

light filtered through a hole
Acclamations seeped out a hole
as if the light had always been known
as if the light had always been loved
we became glowingly curious

How big can light grow
How far can light enter

We yearned to know the barely known
so our eyes sparkled

A folk song began leisurely
then grew into thirst, appetite, and a dry cough
We are little children
imagining the magnitude of light
stretching our necks like chopsticks

we are elderly
Estimating the light's intensity
we elongate like empty cups. We align

We need a hole for money to pour out. A hole for rice to pour out

a hole to breathe
a hole to escape no matter what
Like a punctured rice sack
we array ourselves in a row
As if shutting out the light
a hole expands and expands
but nothing escapes. Like desperate force

nothing enters
Where the light flowed in our eyes
a fine luster flows

We are old souls
We dream and worry
Rolling and welling we dream of worrying

Not even dreaming we are in a blank. Not even
dreaming we are in a dream
a sigh seeped out of a hole

We thought it would come out
We thought it would come in
yet light disappeared
Overflowing yet lacking

we pierced a hole

Like a refrain
like in the middle of the night
we are piercing holes in succession

INCOMPLETE

streetlights stand vertically
their endeavor to break through a plane
completes them
yet feeling lacking
leaves hover only beneath them
it is the soles' job to embroider the roadside
footprints are inscribed like gibberish
perseverance toward home
completes the footprints
when a foot hardly brushes past the leaves
with the crunching sound
they barely curl
until they cannot wither any further

when a body is crushed so is a mind
things you cannot do
things you should not do
things you can do but should not do
literally nothing
works out magically
so a mind grows heavy first
and a body shrivels up
as a mind and a body tilt
a bowl that would bring relief is brimming
yet a mind is crushed without relief

when a mind is crushed a body follows
with the sound of a rib sinking in layers
humans are barely completed

pining for feet
footprints wander vividly
for the point of stagnation and

SWELL

numbers said none
only a hierarchy was there

when people liked the large ones, their eyes glowed red
they raised their bouquets and cheered
when people liked the small ones, their eyes lost focus
they stayed still like microscopes to shrink further

zero grew from zero to hero
decimals never yielded the finale to others

numbers said none

the number of cases
was either imaginary or irrational

real numbers always kept it real
fractions only spilled over

when they failed to grow larger
their glowing eyes lost focus
when they failed to become smaller
their squinted eyes became bloodshot

between two pupils facing each other
like 6 and 9
something was saturated then
flowed down helplessly

depending on where zero is attached
and where a decimal point is marked
some feeling changed 90°
some life changed 180°

something couldn't be grasped even in a lump
some zero gradually descended below a decimal point

some souls of the zeroes were there

DOWNPOUR

a month's worth of events
unfolded within a day
unimaginable things
shamelessly came true

a gambler
spent fortunes beyond his lifetime's keep
a widow
shed tears beyond her lifetime's weep

disregarding its fount a burst water pipe
spouted like a fountain
freshness was fleeting
what ensued was
refreshing agony

no matter how hard I blocked it
something gushed out relentlessly
its name escaped me
no matter how hard I tried
something could never be written

no matter how angsty I was
something could never catch fire

I wanted to touch the treasure
because it was untouchable
I wanted to touch it even more
its shape escaped me
its color escaped me

no matter how much I ate
something carved an emptiness at last
clenching my wormy stomach

I recalled within a day
a month's worth of events
unrealizable things
were shamelessly called up

squeezing through the crack
what endured
what lingered
collapsed
as if nothing more was there

to their delight, they faded like an origin
only unfurled
rhythm persisted

TOO MUCH

was I
beautiful

Stretch out your left arm
Not too wide

You have too many demands
You are depressed

As you stretched out your left arm
air turned to wind
wind turned to wish
Like the eve of a big festival
you blew earnestly

You sway
You are slow and elastic
You are abundant
You roar with abundance

I stand tall
with only one branch
I am bare
Always bare

As if attaching flesh to bones
I think

about me, about you
about the moment I get closer to you

about too much, about the too-muchness of too much, about the moment too much stretches one arm and turns to a tree, about the moment too much finally gains the confidence to grow, about the moment too much stretches its arms into the world, the negative connotation of too much disappears and so

the tree shakes too much

You are too much like yourself
You are too shy so
secrets sprouted shyly in every branch

Too much
you too and me too,
too beautiful

ONE WEEK

it was clear then cloudy
sometimes it rained or snowed
there was a repast then a meal
though I occasionally skipped or overate

evening came and went
yet morning always stayed
plans were barely made then scrapped
though my heart always stayed

it was never filled
like daily tasks
that never get easy despite daily efforts

I put an order on Monday morning
and put a spell on all day Tuesday
I waited on Wednesday
for tomorrow and the day after
like a day that is clear then cloudy
like an evening that comes and goes
when Thursday passes Friday will come

like a meal, evening, or evening meal
I yearned to make absent things present
like weather, plans, or seemingly planned weather
I yearned to gather capricious things in one place

like flickering fluorescent lights
people whose minds are not yet replaced
flocked in from all corners
for they did not want to be extinguished like this

the order we had put in
finally arrived on Friday night
so we could get drunk at last

even if we mess up at work or skip dinner
have no plans or face bad weather
this hour comes
it's fair

see you next time
when we parted it was unfailingly the morning
morning was always there
it's unfair

on Sunday night
we lay in each of our beds
wearing a look of destitution

like opening wallets at parting
we reluctantly
said in a chorus that it's gone

AJEOSSI

Many days I raised hands and gave in
while raising a hand on the lead
In between
I grew older

My bag enlarged
My top thinned
In between
my heartbeat

Nothing to put in
Nothing to take out

Age wrinkles and gray hair
Some things grew in harmony

Books piled up
Memory ran dry
The writing on the journal grew bigger
The writing on the journal looked smaller

When going alone to a rundown restaurant
was no longer a big deal
When it was no great shakes

When I ordered a dough flake soup
spreading my legs wide
wearing glasses down to my nose
dragging my tongue as I read a newspaper

When I scooped the broth with a spoon
opening my mouth like a blurter
I could look back without failure

Like a strand of a colorful sponge stuck in a flake
the boisterous lustrous
back followed; followed back

Laughter courage and phone numbers
Some things dwindled so gracefully

Even though I lied while spattering
my lips always remained chapped

When I put a piece of dough
shutting my mouth without any fuss
closing my eyes firmly
the chewy flour on my tongue is softly

sucked into my deep-seated history
I'm, still, only,
swallowing

I left my bag behind
I didn't use my brain

Ah, just. . . . Shit!

BURST

when you open a body, illness
when you open a mouth, a lie
when you open a window, a thief—a thieving cat pops out

when you open a mailbox, an eyeball
when you open tomorrow, a mirage
when you open a door, a tiger—a paper tiger pops out

duplicity is
what the outside with an empty inside does

THE MASS

when I left home
I embraced heat as always

wrapped in layers of clothing
I couldn't release the heat I embraced
uncontrollable
only my body flared up

I have something fiery inside!
I have something to say!
I have a story to tell you all!

people who didn't want to know my interior
glanced over my exterior and passed by

no one paid attention
so my wit quickly dimmed

to conceal what lay inside
chill air circulated through the square

a precarious line
brushed past my chest

within the layers of clothing
my heart was struggling to beat

when I came inside my house
I couldn't help but envelop heat

it was truly fortunate
that there was a gate
that rumors still lingered within

it was truly fortunate
that I had the key
I opened the door and turned on the light

like an exposed secret
the filament suddenly, snapped

PEOPLE WHO BECOME KIND ONLY AT NIGHT

Anyone can become great It becomes possible when a pronoun and a particle unite
I wasn't confident who I belonged to Anxiety was boiling over in the pot I was struck by an empty stomach and stomachache at once

In the morning I acted surly shaking my head When someone offered their hands I pushed them away I became poor by choice

Anytime you can blossom It becomes enigmatic when a pronoun and a particle unite
I wasn't confident when I belonged I dropped the pot many times because it was hot It easily heated and quickly cooled

During the day I cried like the pot bottom The whole darkened and a spot coal-blackened I became depressed by chance
Night fell

Some people became kind only at night
Recalling the words I uttered today one at a time I flinched and shivered I pulled the blanket over my head in shame I stacked up what I'll say tomorrow in my heart Once again I pulled the blanket over my head in excitement Even in mid-summer I must be covered in the blanket to sleep Only then will I be relieved

I talked as if I were the protagonist It becomes marvelous when a pronoun and a particle unite

Some people became kind only at night
Some people became kind at least at night

Covered in the blanket
unmoving, some people became the night

Part II
From Being to Being

TASTE OF WORDS

don't call me Father Call me Dad
but it's past Coming-of-Age Day
coming of age doesn't mean becoming an adult
you can keep dreaming even as an adult
what if it's a silly dream?
even a silly dream is hard to find when it's needed
all childhood dreams are silly dreams anyway
children are dizzy in harmony
they're dizzy even in moments of spite
but I want to smile like a daisy when it's bright
daisies can't bear fruit and
dizzily they turn white then yellow
yellow then white?
that sounds more beautiful and delicious
suddenly I'm hungry
'cause words are overflowing
thanks to that I'm always out of words
but we're rich

we're poor rich people
we're always deprived of mother's touch
when we feel nostalgic, we should open the fridge
there's dark red fruit!
it looks sour and sweet!
I see it's icy!

we've become rich now
and even scarier
perhaps lightning will strike soon
we should devour the fruit in a flash
we should pick a handful and rinse it right away
'cause taction is different from the feeling of touch
just as black cherries taste different from red cherries
just as not all that's hot is heated
just as how you've just created fruit with words
just as how we devoured it in one breath

down our spines
tangy night sweats started to trickle

the sweet midday waned
like rich rich people
we were earnest and respectable
we were earnestly respectable
our mouths were filled
even without tasting it, we knew

stamping
on the words after the next, the next words
came up our throats

the taste
blew our minds

MAGIC

as if a needle piercing a hole in a black curtain, as if watching a needle thief on the other side through the hole, as if thin light piercing through like a needle, as if sharp light piercing through like a needle, as if the black curtain becoming a transparent mirror, as if the needle thief startled upon his face, as if five minutes into the future turning opaque, as if a black curtain pulled taut

as if the needle thief turning into a cow thief for the time being, as if the hole pierced by a needle turning into a hole dug by a dog, as if the cow thief bolting through the dog hole, as if a heat haze shimmering just in time, as if the atmosphere taking a positive turn, as if the needle thief looking at the mirror with slow satisfied blinks, as if five minutes splitting like rays of light, as if a dog popping in on a single ray of light

woof woof, I cast a spell

when a dog's torso was stuck in the dog hole, when the dog who
couldn't escape winked an eye, when its mediocrity was exposed, when
the black curtain was whipped away, the cow thief
became a cue and fluttered away. Shooting through the curtain

what flowed away flowed back.
Within five minutes
two flows came and went.

When I opened my hand, no sight unfolded.
Something disappeared and something appeared.

The black curtain was never there.
The needle hole was never there.
You just created them all

the coins were always there.
The cards were always there.
You just never knew

words were always there.

seemingly quotidian yet extraordinarily
sometimes striking a stroke in boredom

from being to being
from being to being

transparently like five minutes into the past,
as if flowing
from being to being

GRAMMAR

it starts from a blank

for this room already has many letters
for hardly anything exists
literally
for regularities are rigid
and irregularities ripple
when an unexpected sentence crops up
wriggling through the rift

this room becomes marginally beautiful
this room becomes marginally distinctive
this room verges on an alien land
at last

letters
shadows
the shadows of letters
attain their unique colors
sometimes they elongate like candy sticks
then shrink and vanish into manholes when shy
over them
punctuation glides while embroidering dots

you glare at the spaces between footmarks
with the eyes of a hawk,
you follow regularity

you look at the bare ground without footmarks
with the fin of a dolphin,
you embrace irregularity

you are many

you who love to bicker
you who adhere
but strive to transgress whenever possible
you who wreak havoc when things falter
then readily build them up again
you who sink into a blank and become an exception

with the body of a law-abiding person
and the mind of a lawless person

literally
you enter a certain room
you are scrupulous and unexpected

it is packed with a blank

NECESSARY AND INSUFFICIENT CONDITIONS

Each piece stands well on its own but not as a whole book They don't seem to stand together They're too faceless to face each other They're so estranged that they'd feel strange Pages 23 and 24 don't get along They hate facing each other more than being read On the other hand, pages 48 and 49 long to see each other's faces leaning against each other They yearn to read each other's expressions They yearn to memorize each other's words They yearn to interfere in each other's lives They yearn to become each other's memories They yearn to dog-ear those memories They yearn to stack a part of their bodies on the body of the previous page They yearn to become a part of them They yearn to feel the heartbeat as if they're about to steal a glance They yearn to become a critical moment

The boy loves books He loves expressing He loves to ripple then boil He loves to hesitate when traveling from here to there He hopes to keep this moment dog-eared in his mind He believes he can remember this now and forever On page 23 an unfamiliar word pops up Even before turning to page 24 an unfamiliar word already pops up The split second is distorted The boy grows estranged from this book He lets out a yawn at the same time The boy loves books He loves imagining though not to the point he'd trade sleep for it The boy's finger hates turning from this page The boy's heart hates turning to the next page

The boy closed the book With no mercy

He buried his face in the pillow He closed his eyes tightly Something appeared out of nowhere Something that cannot be hastily named Something that looks like a period lying low on page 82 Something that is pitch-black and jam-packed As if dog-earing tomorrow and dragging it toward today barely in a dream

The boy tucked himself in a blanket A tail began to sprout from a period He took a long breath as if he was standing together Something . . . felt lacking

SURFACE

The ground is bumpy and rugged. The tip of a pen doesn't glide smoothly. A shoe tip turns pointier. Saliva travels down the throat. If you stumble, you must walk from the beginning. If the path lengthens, it tires the walker. An employee is tired. Standing still, you gaze at the trace you left behind. I clump shadows together and put a period mark with it. You collapse as if in lamentation.

To reach the next destination, you must skip ahead. Here and there are in an uneasy relationship. So, let's summon, however. Let's let however lead and take flight. Don't look back and keep on walking. You are obsessed with filling the surface. The backs of your shoes wear down. Your left foot chases your right foot. You are a person who follows yourself. A person who's willingly shadowed.

You and the surface don't act in harmony. Your feet can't keep up with the cleverness of your thoughts. Your thoughts can't endure the silence of your feet. You become exhausted. Like a fatigued spring, you forget your duty. Neither fish nor fowl, you must become him. You are a third-person pronoun. As if leveling the surface, you mark dots. You wipe sweat off your forehead. You voluntarily become unfamiliar.

The end of the surface is out of sight. This sheer fact makes him walk. His beginning renews with each step. Just as some words are said between what was said and what will be said, he is always midway. When he's impatient, he scurries. As if roaring, he remains silent. Ellipses begin to be marked. Saliva accumulates and drools. The words to follow are entirely his.

The surface has hardened. You have come this far. Your shoes are one step closer to being yours. Until the next surface is allotted, you decide to blink like a cursor. Like an ink pen that never dries, you sweat. The person standing on the surface is already tired as he stands. However, he

LIGHT

you are composed of three words
red blue and green

the stingier you get with words
the deeper you bury them in your heart
your face brightens
you gain more words to say

I feel vibrations from your bones
without my knowing
I touch my bones

with a thud
bone joints collide and dig into my eyes
fiery
magenta yellow and teal

though your body is one
what could be you multiplies

when you hide words in your heart's core
joints pile up
bones run riot and

finally they cannot become any brighter
they are dazzling without a single word

I exist in a place that you can never comprehend

as incomplete joints
with no one by my side
even after gathering all the colors
as a heart burning to ashes

without my knowing
as a speck sprouted through me

SALVATION

This poem saved you
This sentence saved this poem
This word saved this sentence

You saved this word
From the depths of water
You lifted up the word, a soul.

You and the word live in symbiosis
Demanding because they are undemanding
Magnificent because they are trivial

Such are beautiful revolutions

Until you revolve
Somewhere on Earth
Until you rove around, spin around, and finally hang around

Until this word
Becomes the language of the otherworld
Until it is yours and yours only

Until you complete this poem
You are beautiful through and through

TRIANGLE

on a plane
an angle is needed
to avoid slipping

a steel bar bends
a stick yields

now you are equal at 60 degrees
equality is manifest in its shape

you refuse to cling
though you want to clang

you need thread though you're not a needle

when you can't clang by yourself
the air stiffens

in a three-dimensional space
you are equally bored at 60 degrees
you desperately need someone to clang you

as the person who clangs you draws near
you grow tense
you want to take flight

the moment a steel bar barely hangs on a thread
the moment a stick quivers and trembles
the moment a clang pierces through the sound
the moment vibration conquers space

on something clear and lofty
a sole crack is drawn

the shape lost its equality for a fleeting moment

EXPRESSION

A baby was sucking milk in its mother's arms. Fervently. Milking it for all its worth. It was wriggling out. Thinking it out. The future, already arrived, was fumbling for the past that lay ahead.

BE YOU

Like the color blue
Love wheeled objects
Be brave but not brash
Never strike a friend first
Nevertheless, repay a blow with double the force

Greet people politely
Listen to your teacher
Get a perfect score on dictation
Never follow strangers
Never cry when you're alone at night
Be honest in your diary
Nevertheless, never write about shameful family matters
Never tell lies

Have dreams
Be grand and advanced but not far-flung
Keep my secret until death
Nevertheless, tell me one of your secrets in return

Cheer for the Korean team
Speak good English
Never obsess over little details
It's all right to lie if necessary
Nevertheless, do tell a lie if it's absolutely necessary
Protect your family

Have a high GPA
Never forsake your dreams
Nevertheless, learn to compromise with reality
Pay attention to what brings in money
Stay away from what wastes money

Always be kind to people around you
Nevertheless, love only me
Be generous only to me

You must excel at everything
Pretend to be good at everything
Exaggerate yourself
Nevertheless, reveal yourself subtly
Know when to let things slide and when to scheme
Read the room skillfully
Roll your eyes skillfully

"Be you" never drained
The following day came with a different "be you"
While moving away from dreams
other obligations snowballed
like a secret to be kept until death

In "be you"
I was absent
so I didn't have to think about what follows

MEDICINE CALLED "IF"

If I had woken up early this morning
If I hadn't missed the subway
If I hadn't spilled coffee on my pants
If I hadn't hastily closed the elevator doors

If I hadn't become a poet
If I preferred emptying over filling
If I preferred silence over conversation
If I preferred picture books over dictionaries
If I preferred morning over the crack of dawn

If I hadn't felt the urge to go out carelessly
If I hadn't been there at that time and date
If I hadn't run into you
If I hadn't uttered those words till the end

If I were used to wiping away your tears not mine
If I were more skilled at looking ahead than looking back
If I hadn't opened and closed each day
with sentences starting with "if"

If I were a better person

When I woke up it was morning
sunlight streamed in
the breeze drifted and
a book I hadn't finished rested serenely beside me

If I hadn't read this book last night

ODD CONJUNCTIONS

Moreover, you broke a cup again. So give me an allowance. Nevertheless, I'm your mom. Still more, I'm your son. Still, I'm hungry. In addition, I'll grow up and become a mom too. Furthermore, you're rich, Son. Because this cup is made of glass. Still, you broke the cup or the cup again. By the way, let me explain the reason. First, I'm the second child. Therefore, we're awkward. For instance, because you're my mom. On the other hand, because I'm your son. Because we are a mother and son or a mother and son. For example, because it's coming up short. Furthermore, I love you. Thus, I broke the cup again. Not only that, I'm your son. Even so, I'm your mom. The former is made of cups. The latter is made of the former. That is, I'm your son! But we're a mother and son! Sure, you were very hungry, Mom. Followingly, I'm your mom. However, I love you. It's just that you're my son as well as my son. Therefore, I'm hungry. Also, because you broke the cup. In short, it's a cup. However, can the pieces gather in one place? Still more, we're a mother and son. As such, we're leftovers. If you're my son. Anyway, I'm hungry and need an allowance. After all, sharing the same blood is an awkward thing. Rather, it's loving but also hungry. On the other hand, we have reached mutual appreciation. That is to say, I'm saying you shouldn't say it. For example, get lost and break the cup. Especially, be conspicuously hungry at this moment. In that case, I'll become the son. And I received an allowance. Nevertheless, I was happy. In other words

SLIP OF THE TONGUE

one person remembers only spoken words
while the other remembers only mistakes

one person remembers only that words were spoken
while the other remembers only their nuances

facial expressions knew
where the spoken words veiled their traces
when mistakes sprouted and would billow
why one person grew cold toward the other
only facial expressions knew

one person and the other
headed toward the same place
then disappeared toward different places

one person and the other
finally merged into one

they walked relentlessly with the same expression

the heart
was nowhere within any of the verses of spoken words

nor upon any rocks along the rugged path

A BOOK

A book that sells A book that sells well A book that wells sell A book with a killer cover A book that kills all the characters A book that suffocates readers A book that's sufficiently mundane from the first page A book that makes readers utterly suffer A book that hits you on the head A book that stimulates your eyes A book that captivates your ears A book that makes your neck stiff A book that pull at your heartstrings A book that bloats your stomach A book that stabs your waist A book that sends chills down your spine A book that turns your ass to pins and needles A book that wobbles its legs A book that makes you pace up and down with a pleading heart A book that tickles the soles of your feet A book written by a famous author A book that reaps the fame it sows A famous book written by an unknown author A book that lives up to its name A book that forgot its own name in the end A book that lost its rationale A book where the author hides behind the work A book where the author takes the spotlight instead of the work An expensive book A book that no one buys A stolen book A book that no one sells A book piled on the display rack A book marred by countless fingerprints A book that everyone reads A book stacked in a warehouse A dusty book A book that nobody ever reads A book the author loves A book only the author loves A book the public loves though the author neglects it A book that has no enemy because it never revealed its innermost self A book that opens its mouth by itself A book that never closes its mouth A book I wrote but does not have me inside A book where page 16 vanished like magic A book where style vanished A book where context vanished A book that vanished from a bookshelf A book that vanished from a library A book banished from a country A book that lost its material properties A book that has become massive dust motes drifting A book that cannot be held or heard A book that exists only in memory A book that is dog-eared multiple times A book that disappeared in silence when I woke up A book that lies around anywhere A book that is not sold anywhere A book that sleeps wordlessly The last book on Earth A newly discovered book A freshly excavated book A book I bought A book I salvaged by opening my wallet, opening my heart A book that finally became a book My book

A PARTIALLY READ BOOK

excuses can be made anytime
stories can unfold beyond a book cover

it's difficult
it's not interesting
it's not my taste
it's out of style
it's different from its title
I missed the right time to start reading
I saw a spoiler
it's made into a movie too
I've been working overtime lately
I'm free now but I don't remember the beginning
I have another book to read in a rush
an author I like better released a new book

how fortunate is it to have a story to pull out and build up

the protagonists in the book want to say something
yet we seal their lips
we are protagonists outside the book
we have so much to say
so we pour out our lines incessantly
pages turn every second in the world beyond the book
but the protagonists in the book hesitate
this might last a while, or forever

with lips sealed
a fully read book says nothing
with lips shut
a partially read book says nothing

no book is partially bought
no book is partially borrowed or discarded
there's only a partially read book

dust collects on the fully-read book
dust collects on the partially read book
amid the layers of everyday dust
memories and amnesia coincide

bookmarks decide to stay still for a while
with lips half-open or half-closed
with the face of those who could eat a horse
with steps adamantly searching for their place

beginnings are met countlessly
endings linger countlessly

once the mind freezes resolutely it doesn't thaw even in springtime

Part III
Transparency Over Transparency

HAND

you reach out
for a white bronze penny
you reach out
for a steamed bun filled with sweet red bean

you reach out to take
you reach out to give

it's possible because you are a twin
it's possible because you are Janus

you hastily pick your pocket
you have nothing to lose

some saddening things make you laugh

you aspired to become a pianist
you aspired to glide on the keys
you aspired to pull strings with sounds

keeping your thumb and pinky apart as far as possible
you moved only between them for a time

there were limits to the expanding world

you stack things up

it's possible because you are a mirror
it's possible because you love yourself

one conceals the other
but not all your embarrassment
as war yearns for peace
as peace can't forget war

you flinch as you linger
what you have done, you already know

for some time
let's agree that only you will know

it's possible because you are human

TOMORROW'S DISH

tomorrow I will always be hungry
hunger swells up like a baking powder
at least for the day that follows
I must sprinkle salt all around
the aftertaste is bitter

today I eat a bowl of rice
my heart stretches like gluten
my skin glistens with fine luster
because I'm thinking of you
I have no time to savor the first taste

yesterday I rinsed the rice
I paid heed and stayed attentive
in pursuit of one noun
I consumed too many verbs
I penned a letter and the sun had set
but nobody came
tears streamed down my cheeks
while thinking of you

rice was preparing to cool down
even before water boiled

DEPARTMENT STORE

None None No mind No money No fourth floor No luck No daughter beside me No time to take care of my daughter My attention wanders No intention to pay attention No contention for paying attention All the free gifts are gone All the bargains are gone The escalator's broken No one's riding the escalator No one's happy about it No movement No one's in their right mind No credit card No discount Of course no late payment My wallet's empty The owner has no expressions No sympathy No disappointment because there was no expectation No truth from the beginning No next direction No time to hesitate yet I can't take the next step No movement at all

There are There are There are people Sparkles in their eyes Heat in their eyes Pairs of blazing and overflowing eyes A broken escalator An emergency exit Pairs of strong or weak legs Pairs of neither strong nor weak legs A working elevator over there A mother who doesn't know her daughter's missing A daughter who doesn't shed a tear though she knows she's separated Ice cream that melts assiduously yet nobody cares Mouths that can eat ice cream Hearts that turn away from ice cream Mannequins dressed in trend-setting clothes Things that haven't come and things that have already come Pairs of widening eyes Pretense Image My attention is all over the place The place will eventually fall apart

Going from the third to the fifth floor
a strange emotion
that can't be known if it's there or not
is there isn't there
is there then isn't there

was there

SECOND WORST

visible diseases and invisible diseases
audible insults and inaudible insults
readable expressions and unreadable expressions

they're bad or
less bad

worse or
all bad

to bad things

a person who opens their eyes
a person who opens their ears
a person who starts reading
bad things

before a book unfolds
a person stands not at the station front
but in front of the station front

a person who's ahead yet takes another step forward
a person who's at the head yet believes there's more ahead
a person who stirs the air like soup
a person who traps themselves in an invisible whirlpool

a person who transitions from a developed disease to a contracted disease

rather than “at the station front”
a person who insists on writing “in front of the station front”
a person who’s ahead yet believes there’s more to write hereafter

visible finger-pointing and invisible finger-pointing
words spoken and words unspoken
lies told and truth untold
by all means they will gladly get worse

even without a scale
a person who tilts to one side
a person who gets busy when their mouth is open
a person who gets even busier as if they’re breaking a tie
a person who gets even busier as if they’re in front of the station front

even the direction they point to
even the strength to move forward
even the speed to gain
even the will to break the tie

were originally in the station
were only in the station

OUR CRAM SCHOOL

once in the school
all the students were seated in the cram school.
we were motionless on the desks
and used in our cram school
like school supplies.
when we use ourselves
are we the subjects or the objects?
the English teacher questioned
though she was unaware herself
though she had been a student
though she had attended our cram school
though she was torn apart like a notebook
breaking like a pencil tip
dragging around crumbs like an eraser
busy gauging surroundings like a ruler.

Korean English math science social studies music arts and physical
education—
there were secrets to good grades but no ethics.
like a notebook without a pencil
like a pencil without a pencil lead
like a pencil lead without an eraser
every hour, minute, and second
were insufficient, were precarious.

yet the world kept turning, and

all our schoolmates who were thrown into society
without mastering social studies
were seated in our cram school
like fully prepared school supplies
clamping our mouths shut
at the last cram school
at the cram school for the last moment
at the cram school that prepares you for death.

we needed only one of these supplies:
worn-out and sickly bodies or the unwillingness to live.
in our cram school
already old or sick
we swarmed like maggots.
friends we met briefly at our cram school
friends who could only see forward or sideways like protractors
became perfect school supplies
compasses that turned 360 degrees
pencils loaded with lead.

like Korean English math science social studies music arts and physical education
that filled our cram school
but were not ours
in our cram school
that was never truly ours

some school supplies
chose not to supply themselves any longer.
some students stepped into the cram school
gladly for the first time
to give up being students here.

the class started.

when we say "we,"
when we transition from the object to the subject
when we become complete without a complement

having evolved into a proper pronoun at last
looking back
we decide to learn ethics in the next life.

PETRI DISH

the science lab had many padlocks
no child had a key
at ten they were too young to own a key
too young to unlock anything
too young to don a white gown
so young that their hands fall silent
even without gloves
so young that their bodies suppress words

the science lab had untouchable things only
no one dared to touch anything

the beaker was empty
the graduation of a cylinder
had no opening to dive in
so the pipette shed drops of silent tears
powders huddled in the mortar and pestle
when the door to the science lab opened unexpectedly
the cover glass became more precarious than thin ice

nothing drew near even when gestured

when the sun set
some people cultivated bacteria
covering one hand with the other

hiding their expressions behind masks
some people touched
things that shouldn't be touched
covering a petri dish with a lid
bending their bodies like a microscope
until they saw things that couldn't be seen

unable to handle them
a child wore a pale expression
tiptoeing outside the window
like a key brought by mistake

he was ten years old

unable to don a white gown
only a white breath wrapped around his body
as if covering a petri dish with a lid
he closed his eyes cautiously

transparency was being cultivated over transparency

FANE

I'm Fane
one day, I introduced myself to myself

feigning to know myself

myself that I was ignorant of
myself that I knew yet desperately feigned ignorance of
because my name is Fane
I momentarily feigned not to be Fane
I only momentarily feigned someone feigning Fayne

in front of a small camera, I feigned loveliness
in front of a big camera, I feigned innocence
in front of a bigger camera, I feigned seriousness

I feigned that the cameras and society were rolling smoothly

I was clearly attending the same school
yet I felt I transferred every single Monday

Good Day, I'm Fane
every time I greeted someone
I felt my name was feigning a good day

feigning kindness to friends
feigning more kindness to teachers
feigning meanness to family

because I had no energy left to feign kindness

I wept tears in the mirror every night
my shoulders were soaked like a towel
they sagged towards the floor like a soaked towel

feigning will become imitating then acting
it will eventually become me

the towel spoke through its soaked fibers
I tried to straighten my shoulders to no avail
they were already clinging to the floor

feigning to be okay I crawled out
feigning ignorance again today I walked past myself

now for the sake of tomorrow
I will go to bed contemplating how to feign kindness

feigning to introspect
feigning to be transformed

an end that begins every day
a beginning that ends every day

I'm Fane
I am repeated every day

A CRITIQUE SESSION

Don't be just kind
Be hurtful at least once

Now, who's gonna start?

Kids were extending their hands
waiting for the teacher's cane

The first hit was relentless

I've seen this passage somewhere
Yeah, it's similar to the second verse of such poet's such poem in such collection
That's exactly what I meant!

Such people and such things poured out all at once

Even a seemingly dense child

carried at least a sharp tweezer, razor, or needle
in the inner pocket of his clothes

It's full of techniques but lacks freshness
It's missing your story
I can't feel sincerity

Sipping a cup of coffee and chatting about love, they were not the kids
with whom I shared today's lunch, snacks, and dinner

Engrave it on your heart
These words will become blood and flesh

An upperclassman who hasn't brought her artwork for some time
An upperclassman who has bulked up from hearing so many words
that became his blood and flesh

The one who is caned
becomes more relentless
One must become callous to not lose this battle of charisma

From now on, it's hand-to-hand combat

Even though it's winter
Even though there's no heating in the classroom
Even though tweezers, razors, or needles might stick out
with flushed faces children take off their clothes
We must find such a person and such a thing!

Don't be kind
Make sure to be hurtful

It seemed they wouldn't survive
if they follow the rules

This is how children learn and grow
Any further remarks?

Only an unquoted mind curled up in the corner of the class

SHOWDOWN

there are people in and out

a person feels uneasy because they're inside
they briefly look out the window
if there's no one outside
they might buy some time

the person inside has nowhere to go in
they feel blocked

like a pile of cigarette butts in an ashtray
they are desolate and worn

a person feels lonely because they're outside
they look up at the building
if there's no one inside
they might be racing against time

the person outside has nowhere to go out
they feel trapped

like ash fell outside an ashtray
they are lonely and heartsick

on the stair landing
where one can go up
or down

a person waits for a person
a person guards against a person

irrelevant to the inside or outside
the walls and doors
stand with senses heightened

GRADUATION SEASON

though my classes ended
I lingered in school
I had nowhere to go

my gleaming diploma will go straight into a drawer
it will accumulate debt day by day

friends intuitively came together
those with a place to go
earned clothes and cars and
attention from the opposite sex
we with nowhere to go
decided to take up a challenge
to sell rice
not our conscience

to take on a task knowing it can't be done
you have to give all your heart and body
we can't help but become invisible

yesterday we imagined the future
today we experienced today
tomorrow we regret yesterday

time

raced at the speed of escaping light or
raced even faster like accumulating debt

right before graduation, one of our friends took time off
right after graduation, one of our friends entered a graduate school

how lucky are we to at least set foot in school

with nowhere to go
we went to a cafeteria to eat

words spilled out when I opened my mouth to eat
someday, let's open a restaurant like this together

an interpretation is better than a dream
if only we could dream a dream

SURVIVAL

one of us will be removed now, right?
we weren't too important
only one was important

the opposite of living isn't dying
it's being removed
my survival
is someone else's removal

starting today you depart from us
you are removed from us

emotions are soluble so
those removed cry from being removed
those not removed cry from not being removed

the roster declares
I will give you exactly a week to mourn

meanwhile
people ecstatic last week that you were alive
might criticize and criticize and
little by little you'd become thin and faint

though you're gone
the survivors form "we"
even with different tastes
different personalities and
nothing in common
because we survived
because we crossed another hurdle
we mourn together for a week

as time passes
we become smaller
we become closer to one

one of us will be removed now, right?
exactly a week later,
we gather our voices and say
the only moment we are truly "we"
the moment you and I swallow our saliva

only one is left
only I am left

Starting today, I have no reason to say "we"

JUVENESCENCE

sojourning as an aspirated consonant
departing as a tense consonant
a sword evolving into a flower
blood evolving into a bone

on certain days
my hand did not move as I wished
for my hand is not I
for my hand is not my heart

freedom was always unnatural

reducing a swollen body
relieving a mind
once again
returning to a plain consonant

I emerged from a dream and stood on the road
and yet, I felt I was on the road within a dream

ADULT

a paper is tearing apart

the sentence starting with "I"
and the sentence ending with "ran"
are splitting between "here" and "there"

where would I belong

if I'm here
I don't have to run
I don't have to go the distance

clutching my empty stomach
I can imagine stories starting with "I"

if I go there
I can find the reason for running
I don't have to guess the ending

I can say "ran" and gasp for air for a while
clutching my full stomach
I can stop the next sentence from popping out

though the paper is tearing
though my two legs are splitting like a compass
though here and there are growing farther

though I can't draw a circle
because there are two centers
though I can't live well-roundedly

though I'm too afraid to dream again
though I'm too embarrassed to conclude early

because the gap grew too big to close my two legs

I ran from here
to there

ORDERLINESS

Latecomers defy signals
The elderly defy laws
For they are the law
self-denial turns into self-renewal
The legal code accumulates exceptions
While neckties shortened
others gasped with necks constricted
For words are watery and their tempers fiery
they could leap at anything anytime
Mindful of when to flow and stagnate
they disguise self-deprecation as humility
Virtue becomes chunky like a rice cake
Whether ignoring your existence or ignoring you
the legal code used ambiguous sentences
even when the law was neutral
Pouring in rather than butting in
while camouflaging deliberation as accidents
they stained Party A and ignited Party B
There was only one mouth so it was easy to muffle it
A red signal showed no signs of changing
The law ossified like customary law then ran wild like bad law
By the time latecomers became the elderly

all the jarring things had become jars
As hard as an iron fortress
they couldn't be struck in haste;
As mushy as mud
no feet could be dipped in comfort

FORM

I was told to appreciate it
so I indulged in it

time flowed by
no one entered
no one left

it was filled to the brim
all particles
turned toward "to the brim"

upon appreciating it
I was demanded a certain form

feelings slipped away from appreciation

those who demanded a certain form
demanded certain formality

seeing deviated from the seen

to form a form
I assumed a good form

playfulness slipped away from appreciation

a few stars hovered on the barren paper alone

HALF OF HALF

I'll give you half
because I can keep the other half

I thought when half and half merge they become one
you thought when one and one merge they become two

I was incomplete
you were replete

amidst drought and flood
we were not free

the one craving to fill
had hope

the one needing to proliferate
had lust

it was half and half

since you were only half
you exhausted it in half a day

trudging back your body
was shrunk in half

you had light in your eyes
a choice in your empty hands
something left to grasp

I still have half left

I cut away half of half and gave it to you
though I knew you'd take it off to eat

like having a crush on half
then crushing it

like half being sufficient when leaving
but insufficient upon returning

you turned away
revealing only half of your body

until you age slightly more than half
you will not remember it
for the yearning to inflate has great inertia
for repayment disobeys consumption

it was half and half

even if I add half to half
you never became one you always
needed another half

no matter how much it is cut in half
I still have
the remaining half
half of half
half of half of half

half that's now the size of a pea
the size of a red bean
as small as dust
so that you can't grab it with your fingers

with that half, I will start again
I will retreat from magnanimous Mount Tai

CONFIRMATION HEARING

Did you write this poem? *I don't remember it well.* What poem were you writing in the spring of 2002? It's all saved on your computer. I have the recently recovered hard disk here in my hand. *I'm not completely denying that I wrote it back then, but to me currently, it doesn't seem to be my poem.* Are you pleading ignorance? *There was a misunderstanding. It's my fault that I wrote a poem that could cause an unnecessary misunderstanding.* Are you admitting that this poem was written by you? *It's a thing of the past. I'm a whole new person now. I'm writing new poems, poems that are appropriate for this era.* I'll take that as your acknowledgment of authorship. I heard there are many problematic poems besides this one. Is that true? *There were such poems, but not all of them were.* Why did you say otherwise earlier? *I relied on my memory, which led me to kind of lie.* Are you saying you even committed perjury? *I was simply following orders from above.* What is "above" exactly? Who is it? *It's my youthful recklessness and carelessness.* Are you going to keep changing your words like this? *My mind was crowded.* Is it true that since you were little, you underlined only subversive words in a Korean dictionary? *My love for the Korean language is the only one to blame.* Is it true that you've been engaging in mischief as a member of "Miss Chief?" *That is a legitimate act. Isn't it mentioned in the Constitution, too? We have freedom of assembly and association.* Are you getting into mischief here and now? *I've already been in Miss Chief.* Haven't these acts of mischief harmed anyone? *It's all due to my lack of virtue. I'll take good care of the people around me.* Don't you realize that there are limits even in mischief? *Childish mischief, dirt mischief, fire mischief, goblin mischief . . . Can I ask what "goblin mischief" is? It seems like I'd have to underline this word.* Are you trying to play with words with me now? *That's not the question I expected.* Are you intentionally avoiding a direct answer now? *I was not in the right state of mind. Could you give me around ten seconds to catch my breath?* Are all poets like you? *I don't understand the question.* Haven't you hurt someone with your poetry? *I deeply regret it in my heart. I feel remorseful.* Won't you deny that this poem is problematic? *There's no problem with it.* Since you claim there's nothing, what exactly is there? *Almost every word has a double-edged sword.* Are you joking with me? *I feel apologetic. I didn't get enough sleep last night.* I will ask once again for one last time. Did you write this poem? *I will confess. Instead of waving a white flag, I will hold a white paper. I will continue to write.*

Part IV
Remaining Words

A ROOM WITH A PLEASANT SCENT – DEAR J

I entered a room with a pleasant scent. I couldn't take a long, deep breath. Fearful that the scents would fly into my body. Fearful that I would steal all the scent in the room. Fearful that the scent would dilute me. Fearful that I would vanish. Fearful that only the scent would prove who I am. Fearful that I would stagnate like a scent, linger like a scent, and vanish like a scent. I felt no one would come if the room with a pleasant scent became a mere room. And only the fact there was a scent would faintly come to mind. In a room with a pleasant scent, "A room with," a pleasant scent said. A room, with a pleasant scent, melded into one.

Leaving behind a pleasant scent, I came out of the room with a pleasant scent. The pleasant scent still lingered around me, lingered in my body. I came out of the room and moved away from it, yet it remained by my side. My heart was operating. I was breathing. My body was reacting. I was panting. I felt I would not vanish even if I entered another room. And I would feel pleasant all the time. And I would smell night and day. I was desperate as if I did not leave enough things behind.

Though I vacated the room, the room still lingered. Though the two of us entered and I came out alone, the scents always endured as scents. Though I subtracted you from me, there still was I. Though I subtracted half, there still was half. A warmth-like hunger lingered. As much as the scent grew distant in my memory, it became clearer that the scent was pleasant. A pleasant scent was becoming a more pleasant scent. An auspicious scent lingered, impossible to erase from "scent." There was a scent. There were scents.

To forget a pleasant scent, I impulsively entered another room. Whichever room I went into, a pleasant scent arduously reeked out. I ardently seeped into the scent. I had come far from a room with a pleasant scent—so far that I forgot where it was—yet a pleasant scent drew near. It dug into my flesh like a gifted scent. "A room with," I said. A room, with I, melded into one. The empty room was flooding with a pleasant scent. Following the direction of the scent, the inside of the room became obsessive.

I saw smoke outside the window. Smoke was emerging from the room with a pleasant scent. As pleasant smoke. Transforming from a reeking to a rising one. Transforming from a room with a pleasant scent to a room with pleasant smoke, I was dispersing. I determined to become vital energy. My body, with my mind, melded into one. They melded into one heart. They melded into one room.

A VERB REVERBERATES

There is a direction There is a flow Here is about to change, changes, changed, will change, will move Here rarely stays here Here tries to escape here A direction pays no heed to a flow A flow does not doubt a direction A verb reverberates Here reverberates together A direction stays constant A flow is smooth Though the inside is boiling burning rotting decaying exploding without damage on the surface it naively flows There is a flow There is a direction A direction does not turn If someone forcibly turns its back it walks backward It flows backward If a headwind blows it walks hunched over It flows hunched over It barely flows It somehow flows The flow rarely changes The flow is unyielding The direction stretches toward that side Though the inside has turned inside out Though the inside is suffering Though the inside is bloated Though the inside is being eaten to the core Putting on a show helplessly a verb reverberates From the enervated side to the energetic side or vice versa From the known side to the unknown side From the infuriated side to the encouraging side From the dispirited side to the spirited side From the persuaded side to the repenting side From here to here From a place that was here to a place that is here And still not enough to a place that will be here again To the direction that does not linger here As if exposing the inside with a heart disloyal to here As if confessing As if throwing everything away without hesitation

There is a direction There is a flow
There is a verb There is reverberation

IMPULSIVE

The scenery outside the window. Dogs are barking.
Four dogs are barking. On four legs they bark.

A person who'll dine enters the restaurant.

A waiter waits beyond the window. For an order to be placed. After the restaurant opened, the menu waited. To be chosen. Even before the restaurant opened, the owner had been waiting. To be successful.
Kindly
They choose the most unfamiliar name. *Give me this one, please.*
Then forget about the timetable. Tear up the diary. Tails scatter in all directions. Yawns and shadows grow longer. As if waiting with their head out,

a person who dines is sitting in the restaurant.
A person who'll dine sits in front of the person who dines.
They signal to the waiter with a glance.
Give me that, please.

The story lengthens. The conversation shortens. Water dribbles from the glass. Rain falls outside the window. Four dogs shake their heads. Like the Four Freedoms*, their barks become fragmented. The tale cracks minutely. There's no need to be smooth. It just needs to flow into the next sentence no matter how.
Life was tough, so even though I knew the rice was cold, I mixed it with cold

water. It was cool and full. It was surging. It was swelling. In that rhythm, I devoured the good old days altogether. The person who'll dine cackles. The person who dines chokes. It's okay to be embarrassed. It just needs to pass through the food pipe no matter how.

The person who dined gets up.
The person who'll dine becomes the person who dines.
To become the person who'll dine,
another person enters the restaurant.
The owner smiles covertly.
The waiter moves overtly.

Ignoring the timetable,
four dogs start smacking their lips.
The person who dined burps.
Nowhere on the menu,
the story concludes.

A different dish was served, not the one ordered. The scenery bustles.
Beyond the window. It becomes.
The person who'll dine says,
This isn't that. As if getting an axe in their head,

the waiter hightails it out of there.
The shadow shortens.
The restaurant door opens like a mouth about to speak.
As if having the first bite of the apple,

the person who was dining disappears into the pages of diary.
As if grabbing a bite and running,
the calculations were done solely in their head.

✻ The Four Freedoms that must be guaranteed to all humanity. The United States President F. D. Roosevelt referenced them in the Annual Message to Congress on the State of the Union on January 6, 1941. They consist of freedom of speech, freedom of worship, freedom from want, and freedom from fear.

SWEETHEART

I met my sweetheart

words came before or feelings hid behind
so our bodies were beyond descriptions

knowledge was strength and ignorance was a cure-all
so we were only vigorous or always intoxicated

too young or too old, we didn't know how to cry earnestly—

each of those mornings
pointing at our puffy eyes
we laughed heartily together

our bodies were heavy but our hearts were light
so our bodies didn't move to our heart's content

I loved my sweetheart
I loved the person who loves

let's take the medicine and get some strength
a word attained a body
as though a body that was not a word
was uttering a word that had become a body
we embodied puzzled looks

to become a body of words
and rescue our hearts
we put on unmatching shoes

we could come in only after going out

SILENCING HANDS

once I muffled your mouth
I was lost for words

I prepare to go out while talking to myself

a hand perfect for sweeping my hair back
a hand elegant when preparing for a performance
a hand expressing me

Nice to meet you
I extend my hand with a bright smile

a hand suitable for holding hands with others
a hand enduring when directing a performance
a hand inscribing the moment

to make a good first impression
I say even unnecessary things
under the table
my clasped hands keep fidgeting

you'd still be covering your mouth with your hands
you'd stay with your mouth shut twice

I remember
every time I lied
your hands
were waving in the air or
struggling to stay afloat

furious
I channeled all the remaining strength into my fist

It was nice meeting you
unable to endure I rose and
extended my whole hand

who will hold
the hand offered in a clenched fist
who will embrace it in their hands

a hand that hasn't met another hand
can't grasp the meaning of empty space

I still haven't opened my fist
because there's nothing inside
because I have no mind to open up
Cheers

when shot glasses or gazes
meet
liquid flows
a heart cracks

on the way home
I looked back
to see if my shadow endured
to see if my footsteps were etched
to see just in case

if there is something to retrieve
even a single drop

could coincide but couldn't converge
the street was always fragmented

FEELING

It's important. To express oneself. It's important. To be replete. To be captivated. To be inerasable. It's important. To give and take. To give with a mouth and take with ears. To give with eyes and to take with eyes. To give them a hand and take their arms. To become absurdly abundant. The feeling

of giving and receiving with a heart is important. The body realizing it. The mind grasping it. The body moving the heart and the mind resurrecting the body. It's important. To embrace. To think with a body and speak with a heart. It's important. To harmonize. To bend at the waist as much as a heart desires. To bend a heart like a body. To open a crack.

In the end, the feeling is important. That you belong. That you can squeeze yourself in. That it's possible. That there's another choice. That this is your territory. That you can do anything as you wish. That you can do nothing as you wish. That you set your heart on becoming a unified heart. That you break your heart and then piece it together.

So, in the end, the feeling is important. The feeling that your privacy is protected rather than actual privacy. The fake that is realer than the real. Pretense rather than nonsense. My seat with an empty plate and a white napkin rather than a slice of cold pizza. My seat that voluntarily cools down when I'm absent. My seat that desperately waits for me.

Let me repeat it. So, in the end, the feeling is important. That justice exists somewhere rather than actual justice. Something rather than *this-thing*. Something that might be useless everywhere or fit perfectly anywhere. Something like a bean loud by itself, bursting unexpectedly amidst the ashes.

Let me say it for the last time. So, in the end, the feeling is important. Feeling rich rather than being rich. Feeling alive rather than being alive. A satisfying sneeze rather than a hundred attempts to clear your throat. That weep-like sound that rages with life, more alive than life!

MACGUFFIN

December 31, 23:59

This world is currently in transit

A shooting star is falling just in time

In a moment my life will start anew
I will start the life anew

I will learn about a secret that will shape the fate of this country
I will become a person who surprises you
I will learn to express emotions I never knew

As I fervently trace the trail of a shooting star
the New Year dawned just in time

I am currently undertaking a critical mission
The finger pointing at the sky is trembling

People who I will surprise
all became protagonists and were surprising me
Despite living each moment, I became a waiting person
Tomorrow arrived yet desire persisted

The protagonists' first word on January 1st was "Ah"

Through transit this world arrived at this world

Grew hungry just in time
nobody remembered the shooting star

SILENT

Who broke this vase?
The kid next door did it

Who taught you to make excuses?
A TV did

Who on earth said that on TV?
I told you, some auntie with permed hair

people searching from afar
gradually closed in and

from close to distant places
from distant to invisible places
they vanished like magic

while passing the buck
I looked around and

I had nothing to blame I utterly
couldn't measure the distance

even though I babbled
a transmission medium stayed silent

something got stuck in my throat while sipping soup
I failed to swallow it down my throat

I did it

though nobody asked
I dropped the spoon
my vocal cords alone heated up

MOONTAN*

A round thing always descended
A round thing occasionally rose

The clamors of drunkards
were turning into ashes In a herd
clouds were swarming in

I too become a drifting cloud and start rolling

We are the people of the night
People who wake up and dream at night
People who face the aftermath at night
People who become heated and
must trigger an accident at night

We are the people who wait
We are the people who roam
We are the people who are always on the move
We are the people charred by emotions
while racking our brains

We are the people who crack jokes at ease
while hardening our hearts

Above the drifting clouds
the moon rose every month
Tearfully and cheerfully

we lean into dreaminess

✽ Moontan: Unlike suntanning, which basks the body to sunlight, "moontan" refers to leisurely strolling while soaking the moonlight.

"HALF," A PITIFUL WORD

spring arrives ever more effortfully
it comes with effort
and vanishes without a trace
like an unserved dish that makes you smack your lips
like a flavorless meal that ended as you smacked your lips

an empty plate is lonely
for excess carries remnants
for remnants carry memories
when it comes to memories
for darkness expires later than brightness

the memory of slicing is vivid
it was sensuous
the moment a plate and a fork collided
the corners of your eyes lifted and became an expression
the moment a knife touched the meat's surface
the corners of your mouth lifted and became a richer expression

whether it was classical or pop
I do not recall
for it blended well with the dining atmosphere
for it was suitable for both silence and conversation
for it flowed only naturally as time

blood trickled out while slicing the meat
unknowingly you smirked
unknowingly I became cruel
like humans
we were humanly blending in

for it was perfect there was little left to do

we halved our words
not by saving laboriously
but by cherishing dearly

we halved our thoughts
not by abandoning hope
but by abandoning habits

something creeps up through our throats
so we sprinkle salt over the soups
not in the mood to sour the atmosphere
but in the mood to scuttle away
as we sprinkle salt we become more sensuously flavorless
we are humanly satisfied

spring revealed only half of itself then disappeared
the urge to express and
the time to contemplate
wavered like heat shimmer

those who averted their gazes
grew pitiful by half
only by half
exactly by half

the remaining words resided somewhere in the heart

HALL

the hall was crowded
there was no one to talk to

a person was in the hall
the hall was with the person

when the hall was lonely
when the hall was alone

when the hall was the loneliest
when people jamming the hall
disappeared altogether

when it became an odd number

in the hall was a person
holes were pierced
where the person was

the hall was embarrassed as if its clothes were holed
it wanted to hole up in the hole

when dishes were rushed out
chandeliers went out
shadows vanished and

silence sank
in the empty space

when it became alone
when its heart moved to its vicinity
unaware that the heart had cooled down

when meantime fluttered away
and the hall was swallowed into the hole

the hall alone
became a gigantic hole

there was a hall
the hall was in a person

VAMPIRIC

You all resemble me. You all are small and resemble me. You all are small and resemble me obsessively. You all used me as a reference. You all created me. As though we took shares and separated from one body, I resemble you all. I am big and resemble you all. I am big and resemble you all fiercely. You all are confident like the originals. Like a mirror. I am perplexed like a duck claw. Like someone who looked in a mirror. (Unwittingly) I suddenly become small. I shrink. I wither. I crack. I become excessively like you all. I drop out of the formation you all made. I have lost my qualification. To resemble. To like. Lacking confidence, I could not even resemble myself. My bones emaciate. My fat dissolves. I wear away. Now you all are small, and I am even smaller. If you all become smaller than me, I will be perplexed. Each cell will go nuts. It will go to the extreme. It will swallow saliva and close its eyes. (Pretending it is none of your business) you all smack your lips and start sucking each other's blood. You all are small and so eager to live. I am even smaller and so wretched. It's strange. I'm losing weight, emaciating, turning pale. I am gradually moving away from myself. I become unfamiliar. And you all even smell. The smell I dislike, the smell that is small but big, my smell. Small and big smells depending on the parts. I pull myself out again. I pluck out my tongue and extract the cochlea I have tucked away. My pupils dilate like hollow caves. A mucus flows out of my nose. (Ignoring it) parts are all different. Big parts, small parts, neither big nor small parts. Parts that resemble me more, parts that resemble me less. You all raised me up. It was you all who supported me. It was none other than you all who created me. I turn my back on tomorrow and approach yesterday. Like a noon shadow, I voluntarily shrink. I become firm. I become dense. Resolutely, you all add the compressed me as an attachment. The me that does not feel like me. Parts of me I never knew existed. Blood drips from my smaller body. You all, who are less small, smack your lips. The mirror shatters. I despair over hope more than before. I hope for despair less than before. You all are big and laugh raucously. I am small and whisper softly. (It's fine if you don't know but) you all, who resemble me and thus are unfamiliar; you all, who are like blood, like blood-cells . . .

TIME LAG ATTACK

a person waiting
a thing coming

the moment time cracked
the time a moment shone

time is brief
and a moment is scarce

so the crack made room
and the shine formed a pattern

time is not crowded
and a moment is dizzying

so I've slipped my foot into the crack
enchanted by the patterns I've been speckled with dots

a thing waiting
a person coming

a door opened
air blew in
carrying an anecdote several words followed

within one body
an overlap occurred

time used to be a mere moment
a moment used to swamp time

a door opened and closed

even after it came and went
a movement still awaited

a replete sense of loss prevailed

OPEN

I opened them
I opened the locked door
I opened the side door and the front door opened
I opened crock pots
in the corner of the yard
I opened ruins archaic
like a conflict
Corners emerged like the center
Someone with a booming voice opened a class reunion
Someone skillful
opened a fish belly
as if boasting
Someone opened a pot
as if flipping eyeballs
Anything opened like everything

Someone tearful opened a year-end gathering
Someone with many stories opened their mouth
All the gathered people listened intently
Someone tearful opened their heart
Opened stories evoked zealous cheers

Someone tearful
opened the word "open"
Like a blooming flower

opening opened
That an opened thing can open again
that a fully opened thing can open further
was astonishing

It opened
The fever opened
Nine out of ten
contained heat poured out
Someone with many stories
fervently opened a circumstance

Carelessly like a curtain
wide like a window
audaciously like a question it opened
Then like a custom
an outmoded thing zealously opened
Like a door to a room
a thing resembling a heart
used to open every day

There were many places to frequent
but nowhere to settle

Like a lie
a new era opened
Like a beggar
nothing changed

A lid opened
like a convenience store at the first dawn
It was abundant yet poor

Like handcuffs
I couldn't open many things
Like a wallet
I couldn't open anything

My eyes suddenly opened wide
My hands started fidgeting

Finally a path opened
Like a berry
tears formed and ripened

THE REST

I love an alley
I love dawn

for there's no one

I end up here
my eyes are drawn here
my feet lead me here

even without a push

I'm here when I wake
I'm speaking by surprise
as if whispering or murmuring
I'm calling

I see the rest
a small thing attracts a small thing

the rest gathers
it becomes the larger rest
it becomes a lonely lump

an alley fills up
dawn overflows

with a body alone but many
with a mind many but alone

gladly blending into the rest
lingering as an unfulfilling part
contemplating what to say next

I almost utter something but hesitate
I omitted the town square
I let the morning slip away

I am in the alley
I am in the dawn

no one is here
I am here

COMMENTARY: PLAY AND REVOLUTION BY KWON HYEOK-WOONG

1. A lunchbox bomb exploded

On a lovely day, men and women gather for a picnic. They sit in a grassy field in a forest, chattering idly. The men don suits, while the women are either dressed in lingerie or are undressed. Beside women's clothes, bread and fruit from a picnic basket are scattered around. This is Édouard Manet's famous painting *The Luncheon on the Grass* (1863). At the time, this painting drew severe criticism for deviating from classical beauty standards in its figures and colors. One woman sits undressed among men, gazing at the viewers. The lighting on her is not illustrated through conventional shading techniques. According to common sense at the time, light should gradually darken from a bright area. However, Manet believed that, under bright light, we perceive a subject in terms of bright and dark parts rather than in gradations. As a result, the woman became the subject portraying the reality of saggy belly fat (She is an ordinary woman next door, not the goddess of beauty) and the factual nature of light (In contrast to the traditional gradation technique, which reveals the unnaturalness of three-dimensional vision, the gradation here demonstrates the naturalness of two-dimensional vision). Furthermore, her gaze does not leave us, the viewers, in anonymity. Instead of us merely looking at the painting (We exist simply as bodiless gazes at this moment), it goes above and beyond: It gazes back at us (We are now bodies captured by her gaze). Moreover, this painting abandons a one-point perspective. The boat above the man's head on the right appears excessively small compared to the woman. But think about it. Our focus is on her, so would we even notice such an insignificant detail as the boat? *The Luncheon on the Grass* triumphed over criticism that labeled it as "obscene," "vulgar," and "barbaric," exposing the hypocrisy of the bourgeoisie of the time. The painting unveiled the reality of 19th-century Paris, as well as the burgeoning prostitution industry that propped up the ideals of bourgeois art. The woman is illuminated by the same light that shines on prostitutes in shop windows, and her gaze scans the bodies of men exposed to the prostitutes' solicitation.

Nonetheless, it has now become clear that the subversive aspect of *The Luncheon on the Grass* should be subverted once again. Firstly, men are dressed in suits, so why are women undressed? As manifested through the clothing, the notion that men inherit civilization while women belong to nature is imperialistic. First, civilization must conquer nature; second, colonies must come under the protection of an empire; third, women must submit to men. This is a three-layered strategy as well as a three-layered shackle. *The Luncheon on the Grass* fails to expose the unnaturalness of this structure. To dismantle this fundamental structure of desire, the luncheon on the grass must be entirely dismissed. Let us imagine the following: During the cheerful wanderlust, the picnic basket opens. Instead of bread and fruit, a bomb explodes—the lunch box bomb of Yun Bong-gil [1]was hiding in the basket of this painting.

---

1 Yun Bong-gil was a Korean independence activist. He set off a bomb Hongkou Park in Shanghai in 1932. (Footnotes throughout this commentary are written by the translator unless otherwise noted.)

Oh Eun's poetry is a modern-day lunchbox bomb. It is another kind of excitement that transforms a lively picnic into a scene of chaos; it is another form of subversion that subverts subversive poetry. This statement may seem nonsensical, but even Oh Eun's most sensical poems are less sensical than this assertion. And few poems have simultaneously received vehement criticism and fervent praise like Oh Eun's. Certainly, several senior poets have navigated through this sea of criticism and acclaim. Hwang Byungsng, Kim Haengsook, and Jo Yeon-ho all have. Yet, once their endeavors went through serious evaluation, their works were acknowledged as significant achievements in contemporary poetry. Hwang Byungsng's dramas (featuring countless fictional characters) consist of confessions in a lyrical style. Kim Haengsook's narrative style (freely combining literary and colloquial languages) stems from the exploration of the binary aspects—cognitive and emotive—of language. Jo Yeon-ho's non-sentences (which are either classist or pseudo-scientific) are expressions that necessarily emerge when pursuing infinitesimal meaning. Oh Eun's poetry does not follow any of these precedents. He constantly initiates play in his poetry; there is nothing but play. Because poetry consists of words, he takes wordplay for granted; this play is nothing but wordplay. And Oh attempts to start a revolution through this play. In fact, for him, play itself is a revolution. Can the hybrid of play and revolution succeed? Oh Eun's success or failure rests on this very question.

2. The Narrative of the Surface and the Narrative of the Hidden

Every language necessarily carries a "thing to be conveyed," but this does not always align with the "thing actually conveyed." We refer to the pure concept that requires no medium of transmission as an "idea" (ἰδέα). Paradoxically, everyday conversation models are built on pure concepts that do not demand any expression–in other words, inexpressibility. As demonstrated by politicians and lovers who habitually lie or make an empty pledge, all misunderstandings and nuance stem from the gap between a thing to be conveyed and the thing actually conveyed. Poetry, too, relies on this difference. Poetry grows, gathering energy from the gap between the thing actually conveyed and the thing to be conveyed. In poetry, the "thing actually conveyed = surface" is not just the manifestation of the "thing to be conveyed = what is hidden." Poetry speaks twice: once from beneath the surface (also the case for oratory, editorials, legal documents, and newspaper articles) and once again from the surface (unique to poetry).[2]

Oh Eun pushes this surface to its limit. So to speak, he stretches this surface to the surface of the surface. Intention (the hidden side) and expression (the surface) pertain to a statement, yet Oh divides the

---

2 In my essay "Poetry Speaks Infinitely" (Position, Winter 2014), I illustrated how poetry is divided on the surface in five ways: ① by being unnamable, ② by not delivering a message, ③ by being uncommunicable, ④ by leaking out, ⑤ by not being in the realm of consciousness. Each of these resists ① schematization, ② communication, ③ opinion, ④ intention, ⑤ consciousness, respectively.— Kwon

surface of expression into statements and signs. He then subdivides this second surface (sign) into the hidden side (signified) and the surface (signifier), constructing narratives at the level of signifiers. If we call a typical story built on meaning, "the narrative of the hidden," it would be fitting to label this special story constructed from the level of signifier, "the narrative of the surface." In the narrative of the hidden, signifiers are nothing but tokens to summon the signified, discarded once the signified is summoned. Tokens are prophecies about future events, thus unactualized in the present. They are akin to promissory notes drawn in advance, merely signifying promises for the future. Through this prolonged process of summoning and discarding, the chain of signified—concepts that cannot be actualized, specters without bodies—momentarily reveals its appearance. In the narrative of the hidden, the signified controls the signifiers, and this is different from the narrative of the surface. In the latter, signifiers themselves are the signified. This is because, from the beginning, signifiers are the signifiers of signifiers, i.e., the signifiers that manifest the thing that has revealed itself as signifiers. In the narrative of the surface, the signifiers control the signified.

> If you are sad and like beer...
>
> Let's go to Mosk Bar.[3] If we go to Mosk Bar, we can meet Viktor Tsoi, the best singer of the time. Only Heidi is the singer of Gene Bar, and she only sings yodel.[4] Liquors at Warsza Bar are too expensive,

---

3 In Korean, "v" is pronounced as "b," and "r" at the end of the word following a vowel is silent. In other words, "va," "var," and "bar" are all pronounced as "ba"

4 In Korean, based on the same mechanism mentioned above, "Mosk bar" and "Gene bar" are pronounced the same as "Moskva"(Moscow) and "Geneva."

so you should pay Istan *bul* for a shot of Whiskey.[5] At this point, it's only natural that we go to Mosk Bar. To go to Mosk Bar, we need a car first. Over Casablan car or Alas car, I recommend Sri Lan car, which has been varnished. When you drive Sri Lan car and follow Os-ro,[6] you reach Amster dam.[7] When you press Isa bell, nine times out of ten, three Bre men will come out. The one with Mona *ko*[8] has a bad temper, so avoid him. The empty-headed man wearing Québag has no power. The last one is probably eating Kath mandu diligently with his four arms.[9] Evenly sprinkle ready-made Peloponne sauce over mandu. You can also offer him a Gothen barley drink cultivated in Leba *non.*[10] When the man becomes jubilant and gives you Helsin Key, you're halfway there. When you open the small door of the dam with Helsin key, you'll see Cairo over Cam bridge. It's during the monsoon season, so Bah rain or Nairo *bi* might be falling.[11] You can't walk there because Singa formalin is flowing down.[12] Let's rent a Ro *ma*[13] or Münc hen at the entrance of Cam bridge. A cussing granny must be eating wet red bean with Edin butter while watching Vladivos talk show. It's hard to entice her with just a couple of Phnom pens or a Monte video. Start a fiesta while the granny shouts new *yok* such as "M *yanma*"

---

5 "Bul"(불) refers to a dollar.

6 Korean "ㄹ" is distinct from "l" or "r" in English, and both alphabets are transliterated in "ㄹ." "-로," which indicates a street, is officially transliterated as "-ro."

7 "Dam"(담), pronounced "d-ah-m," means a fence.

8 "Ko" (코) means a nose in Korean

9 "Mandu" (만두) means dumpling.

10 In Korean, Gothenburg is pronounced as "yeh-te-bo-ri" (예테보리). "Bori" means barley. "Non" (논) means a field for farming.

11 "Bi" (비) means rain in Korean.

12 "F" is pronounced as "p" in Korean

13 "Ma" (마) is hanja-style vocabulary for a horse.

at your face. That is, strike Bei *jing* or Chica *go*.[14] The startled old woman would surely lend them to you with no objection. Oh, and you should check Ro *ma* or Münc hen well before riding them because you'll most likely regret it if you just Jakar ta.[15] This is because some of them can't run well as they are stricken with Buda pest. When you're halfway through Cai-ro, you'll see Antananari *bo*, which supplies water to Pra *ha*.[16] There, a humongous Pala *u* or Ba *hama* might be chewing Al Jelly while singing Tong *ga*.[17] By fair means or foul, buy Qa tar from arrogant ye men who are patrolling the compound. You must collect Qa tar there because you'd need to pay them ka *bul* or Papua New guinea in other places.[18] Now, we only need to pass through the cave at the end of Cai-ro. It's not that thrilling because the light is always coming in. In front of the Mosk Bar outside the cave, flies would be swarming in to see Victor Tsoi. When your turn comes, squeeze their *fiji* a little bit or present Bru cells.[19] That's your ID tonight. When you enter Mosk Bar, Viktor Tsoi will appear faintly through the thick cigarette smoke.

---

14 "Yok" (욕) means curse words in Korean. "Yanma" (얀마) is an aggressive way to call another person. "Jing" (징) refers to a gong, and "go" (고) refers to a drum.

15 The original text plays with "ta," the root of "tada" (to ride). However, "Jakar ta," as a whole, does not have any meaning in Korean and is thus nonsensical.

16 "Bo" (보) means reservoir, and "ha" (하) means canal.

17 "U" (우) is hanja-style vocabulary for a cow, and "hama" (하마) means a hippo. Algeria is pronounced "Aljeri" in Korean. "Ga" (가) means a song.

18 See footnote 4.

19 "Fiji" is pronounced the same as "piji" (피지), which means sebum or whitehead.

> Hand Qa tar you bought earlier to Nor wayter, and he will roll a cigarette for you. If you don't like beer, you can drink *hoju*, *cheongju*, or On the Rocks Wisskey.[20] At Mosk Bar, it doesn't matter if you sell things or not. "I'll play Milford Sound," says Viktor Tsoi, who's admired by many youngsters. "I'll play it in delhicato. To those who chase after power, just give Viagra. To us, give freedom...[21]

The names presented in the Arial script in the quoted narrative denote specific locations on Earth. However, in the narrative of the surface, these names serve as the signifiers that are liberated from the signified. As signifiers, they create new signification. Moscow, Geneva, and Warsaw are the names of bars, while Casablanca and Alaska are the names of cars. This concept applies beyond nouns. Sydney is part of "because the light is always coming in," and Greece is part of "It's not that thrilling."[22] Like this, a total of seventy-three cities are named. These are unique examples where the signifiers act as the signified,

---

20 In Korean, Australia is often called "Hoju" (호주), and "cheongju" refers to refined rice wine as well as a city in South Korea. "Ju" is a suffix for an alcohol, as in "maekju" (beer) or "soju."

21 Oh Eun, "Wordplay Improv–Viktor Tsoi is in Mosk Bar," The Pigs of Hotel Tassel, Minumsa Publishing, 2009, 15-17. – Kwon; Other than the names marked in the translation, the following places are mentioned in the original text. These names were not translated because the puns could not be emulated without causing much confusion due to the linguistic difference: Nice (a city in France), Wien, Nepal, Lima, Mali, Hong Kong, Saipan, Bogota, Ghana, Oman, Sudan, Samoa, Sydney, Greece, Paris, Busan, Panama, and Granada.

22 In Korean, "is always coming in" is a wordplay of Sydney (hangsi deuni 항시 드니; hang Sydney). "Not that thrilling" is a wordplay of Greece (geuri seuril... 그리 스릴......; Greece ril...).

and, remarkably, we get to tour the world as we navigate through this chain of signifiers. In the end, this poem tells us two stories. One is the quest for Viktor Tsoi in "Mosk Bar," linking the city names through the play of the signifiers. The other recounts the journey around the world, with the city names constructing a path to Moscow following the shadow effect of signification. In this poem, the signifiers transcend the dominion of the specter known as the "signified" and become double symbols that, as signifiers, carry the signified. Some of the poet's surface–narrative craftsmanship is made evident as follows:

First, using idioms idiomatically.

> In the summer, they whispered love around the clock. Whenever the man cried for the moon, the woman turned up her nose at him and laid a smoke screen. She was no small deal. Her teeny-tiny hands and velvet voice were enough to steal the spotlight. While the man and the woman were head over heels in love and biting each other's head off, children resembling sparkling gems or roly polies burst into laughter and danced to the tunes. At last, the awkward scene became well-orchestrated. Each time the woman buttered him up, the man became yellow-bellied.[23]

Idioms are usually called "dead language" due to their fixed usage and meanings, making it difficult to infuse vitality into them. However, Oh composed this poem entirely using idioms. In the quoted passage alone, there are as many as seventeen idioms. As these once-lifeless idioms

23 From "The Change of a Season–certain wordplay made up of idioms," ibid. p. 32. – Kwon

form a long chain, the story, which might have been nothing more than a mundane drama, becomes vivid. The poet achieves this by using idioms as single units. Phrases like "teeny-tiny hands" or "velvet voice" are idiomatic expressions where two nouns are joined through simile, and no new meaning is created within the phrases.[24] However, when these idioms become the units of the surface narrative, they function as signifiers. Consequently, the whole story becomes disconnected from the clichéd context. As such, this craftmanship can be summarized as follows: using idioms idiomatically to transcend their idiomatic usage.

Next, utilizing a dictionary.

> Today, once again, you play with words. Chatter, chatter. If you stumble along the way, you take a sip of water. Gulp, gulp. Then, you play with water. Splash, splash. If you get hungry along the way, you drink gruel. Lickety-split. Then, you play with taste. Munch, munch. If you're full along the way, you play with your body. Hop, hop. Then, you play guard dog. Eager beaver. If you catch a thief along the way, you show off. Sparkle, sparkle. Then, you play nothingness.
> When you are bored from not playing, you play with a door. Click, click. If you get sleepy along the way, you play with a dream. Wriggling and squirming.
> Then, in your dream, you play with a horse. Clip clop. If you feel nauseous while riding a horse along the way, you play with a blood vein. Thump, thump. Then, to come to your senses, you play in

24 The literal translations of the two Korean idioms are "hand like a fern" and "voice like nightingale's."

> water. Huff and puff. If your hair gets entangled along the way, you play several games. Nine out of ten. Then, you play mind games. Growing and billowing. If you get hungry again along the way, you make up your mind with peace of mind. Over and over. Then, you play in a pond.
> Feeling it is unfair that you cannot play, you play with ㅁ. You enter a mouth (ㅁ) and will not come out until someone tosses you a ㅂ.[25]

To engage in "ㅁ play," you need a Korean dictionary. The extensive chain that unfolds with "mal-mul-mieum-mat-mom-mang-meot-mu-mun-mong-mal-maek-myeok-myeot-mam-maeum-mot (word, water, gruel, taste, body, lookout, style, nothingness, door, dream, horse, vein, swim, some, mind, heart, pond) is the outcome of exploring the "ㅁ" section of a Korean dictionary.[26] The narrative of the hidden is constructed from a chain of meanings. A chain of meaning is grounded in causal judgment, and causal judgment is based on the "intention"—assumed to carry the signified—of the speaker. Everything is contingent on hidden intentions, the very things we say are concealed in our minds. In contrast, there is no such order of meaning in a dictionary. What exists instead is a meaningless array of signifiers, which appear to be arranged in order. There is no inherent meaning or intention in "ㄴ" following "ㄱ," or "ㅑ" following "ㅏ." This is purely conventional. Following a dictionary liberates signifiers from intention and subjects

25 Oh Eun, "ㅁ-play," We Love the Atmosphere, Munhakdongne, 2013, p. 11. – Kwon

26 ㅁ is a Korean consonant equivalent to the sound of "m." All of the words listed in the parenthesis start with ㅁ.

them to an unintentional order. When these symbols take on meanings, as in the third stanza, "ㅁ" becomes a mouth, and "ㅂ" becomes a horned "ㅁ." In other words, the signifiers in the third stanza are pictographs of a kind. Even on a completed surface like this, additional narratives emerge. You started playing with words, and while speaking, you got thirsty and drank water. Amid playing in water, you got hungry and drank gruel, and it was tasty . . . and the story continues. "Along the way" and "then" appear in each sentence to connect the narrative, but, as you know, there is no true causality because there is no underlying intention. The process of this play resembles the meaningless yet well-ordered arrangement in the dictionary."[27]

Next is utilizing a manual or calendar like a dictionary.

> In January, I felt as if everything would go well
> A total disaster lasted until yesterday
> The drunken gibberish of last month has all vaporized
>
> In February
> I blame the cold
> for not departing
> One day I suddenly wanted to eat chocolate

---

27 Wordplay using polysemy also follows the arrangement of a dictionary. This is because Oh arranges headwords following the order of a dictionary. For example, in "Seol" (from *We Love the Atmosphere*, p. 10), "seol" is transformed to tongue, excretion, disclosure, leakage, Lunar New Year, and snow [These words contain "seol"—translator]. – Kwon

In March
I want to buy a bag for no reason
I want to have more items with my name on them
I want to become cherry blossoms and let my name bloom
One day I suddenly wanted to buy candy

April is not as cruel as I thought
There's only one reason:
I died a long time ago

In May, I have an identity crisis
I am not a worker
I am not a child
I am not a parent
I am not a teacher
nor am I coming of age
Who am I, really?

What facet of myself may I celebrate?[28]

This is not a narrative of any particular year; rather, it represents a recurring year. If it were the narrative of a particular year, this would have been the narrative of the hidden. Actions outlined in a manual or events marked on the calendar follow a fixed order, so they are detached from causal judgment. In January, there was a fresh start, implying that the previous year was a total disaster with never-ending year-end parties, leading the speaker to speak drunk gibberish for many

28 Oh Eun, "One Year," ibid, pp.115-6.— Kwon

days. In February, the speaker's resolution lasted only for a few days due to the cold. Valentine's Day was in the middle of it. Come March, the speaker wanted to become a student again and have an entrance ceremony. . . . And the story continues. However, as the story unfolds through anniversaries, it exposes an ordinary citizen's same old life—lifeless as death. The speaker, who lived through the year died in April. This statement is possible because April begins with April Fools' Day. Yet, this is also a declaration that this land is a wasteland even more so than Eliot's proclamation.[29]

A discussion on the poet's craftsmanship could go on indefinitely. In the last two volumes of his poetry collections, it can be said that each poem introduces a new methodology of signifier–narrative craftsmanship. This is the revolutionary power of Oh Eun's wordplay. If what we named "the narrative of the surface" is the game that dismantles and rebuilds the world, what else can it be but a revolution? This is not an unsophisticated play. Now, it's time to delve into this poetry collection.

---

29 The poem ends by talking about January of the following year, but a line sneaks into it: "Thinking about the five Sundays in February, his Excellency is happy" (p. 117). Only until the government of Roh Tae-woo [commonly considered the last dictator of South Korea—translator], the presidential inauguration was designated as a public holiday. Therefore, his Excellency is the mockery of a soldier-president or dictator. The only one who was happy on that day was the president.— Kwon

3. Dark Language

Scientists have discovered that the atoms we can observe make up only 5% of the universe's total energy. The remaining 26% is unknown matter responsive solely to gravity, and 69% comprises unknown energy working against gravity. These unknown components are called "dark matter" and "dark energy," respectively. "Dark" is a fascinating metaphor representing the concept of the unknown or unknowable. Following this, let's label Oh Eun's signifier that advances the narrative of the surface as "dark language." Just as dark matter and energy are the actual matter and energy that operate in our universe, dark language is also an actual language that operates in our poems. Just as dark matter is indirectly discovered through a gravitational lens and the rotational speed of stars in galaxies; just as dark energy is indirectly calculated through the expansion of the universe; dark language can also be gauged by the distortion of certain spacetime.

> once in the school
> all the students were seated in the cram school.
> we were motionless on the desks
> and used in our cram school
> like school supplies.
> when we use ourselves
> are we the subjects or the objects?
> the English teacher questioned
> though she was unaware herself

though she had been a student
though she had attended our cram school
though she was torn apart like a notebook
breaking like a pencil tip
dragging around crumbs like an eraser
busy gauging surroundings like a ruler.

Korean English math science social studies music arts and physical education—
there were secrets to good grades but no ethics.
like a notebook without a pencil
like a pencil without a pencil lead
like a pencil lead without an eraser
every hour, minute, and second
were insufficient, were precarious.

yet the world kept turning,

"All" students went from a school to a cram school. Oh Eun likens these students to "school supplies," and the college entrance exam retakers are indeed supplies for society. A spatiotemporal movement like this recurs. Explaining the difference between "we" and "us," the English teacher is unaware that she and her students are in the same position. She, too, was a student and an exam retaker. Moreover, she, too, was nothing more than a "pencil tip, eraser, ruler, and notebook," consumed and depleted. Are we, including the teacher, playing the role of the sentence subject, or are we mere objects being consumed and depleted? Every moment is precarious, giving rise to this question. However, despite the waste, consumption, scarcity, and deficiency—or, to be precise, unrelated to these—the Earth keeps spinning. If Galileo's murmur was a conviction about the truth, the addendum of this poem is the proclamation of harsh reality. *No matter what happens to you, the world will keep rolling. Because moral virtues are not taught in cram schools.* Two displacements occur: spatially (from school to cram school) and temporally (from being a high school student to being an exam retaker; from being a teacher to being an exam retaker and back to being a student). This is mischief, chaos, and stunt, of the hidden dark language. This is the emergence of facts caused by spacetime distortions. And this is how the poem concludes:

> when we say "we,"
> when we transition from the object to the subject
> when we become complete without a complement
>
> having evolved into a proper pronoun at last
> looking back
> we decide to learn ethics in the next life.
>
> —Excerpt of "Our Cram School"

When classes complete us; when we become the sentence subjects and leave the cram school; when we view ourselves as independent because we no longer require assistance—we become pronouns in these exact moments. Ethics is irrelevant in this round of life. We are not subjects but rather subjects that have become objects, i.e., shadowy figures that can be replaced by anyone. Dark language twists the language of the surface to expose the underlying distortions. Hence, unlike its playful surface, it becomes a language that vehemently criticizes ideology.

> "Be you" never drained
> The following day came with a different "be you"
> While moving away from dreams
> other obligations snowballed
> like a secret to be kept until death
>
> In "be you"
> I was absent
> so I didn't have to think about what follows
>
> –Excerpt of "Be You"

The suffix "*-daum*" is attached to a noun or a root word, indicating that a particular object possesses its innate features in a "sufficiently or positive" manner.[30] The judgment of whether something is "sufficient or positive" is in itself an ideology, as it involves evaluation. But who evaluates? It is the ideologues who assert themselves as legislators. This poem enforces various "*-daum*" as imperatives that alternate between obligation ("you must") and prohibition ("you must not"). However, these commands come with numerous exceptions and conditions. It unfolds as follows:

---

30 For example, "*namja-daum*" refers to qualities that are conventionally—or "sufficiently or positively"—masculine, such as courage and strength. Because English does not have a suffix equivalent to "*-daum*," the poem was translated as "Be You" according to its context, in which "*-daum*" statements ironically urge you to be you (e.g., as a boy).

"Never strike a friend first / Nevertheless, repay a blow with double." (1st stanza), "Be honest in your diary / Nevertheless, never write about shameful family matters" (2nd stanza), "Keep my secret until death / Nevertheless, tell me one of your secrets in return" (3rd stanza), "Never forsake your dreams / Nevertheless, learn to compromise with reality" (5th stanza), "Always be kind to people around you / Nevertheless, love only me" (6th stanza), "Exaggerate yourself / Nevertheless, reveal yourself subtly" (7th stanza). Through these conditions and exceptions, the obligatory and prohibitory commands become privatized. The criteria for judging all "*-daum*" are not universality but personal interests. As personal interests are incessantly renewed, "*-daum*" never wears out. As everything is a pretense, there is no me in "*-daum*." As it is intangible and thus uncountable, nothing follows "*-daum*." By distorting the narrative of the surface, dark language reveals these sinister intentions coiled deep in the narrative.

"Idea" (ἰδέα) and "ideology" are cognate. When what is "intended to be conveyed" (but cannot be adequately conveyed) is conveyed in the narrative of the hidden side, an idea transforms into an ideology as follows.

> Latecomers defy signals
> The elderly defy laws
> For they are the law
> self-denial turns into self-renewal
> The legal code accumulates exceptions
> While neckties shortened

others gasped with necks constricted
For words are watery and their tempers fiery
they could leap at anything anytime
Mindful of when to flow and stagnate
they disguise self-deprecation as humility
Virtue becomes chunky like a rice cake
Whether ignoring your existence or ignoring you
the legal code used ambiguous sentences
even when the law was neutral
Pouring in rather than butting in
while camouflaging deliberation as accidents
they stained Party A and ignited Party B
There was only one mouth so it was easy to muffle it
A red signal showed no signs of changing
The law ossified like customary law then ran wild like bad law
By the time latecomers became the elderly

all the jarring things had become jars
As hard as an iron fortress
they couldn't be struck in haste;
As mushy as mud
no feet could be dipped in comfort

—"Orderliness"

"The elderly" are sly old foxes. They violate the law because they themselves are the law. The law is something they apply, not something applied to them. In the same line of reasoning, those who establish the law exist outside the law, not subject to its application. Nothing is as unlawful as the logic behind legislating or drafting a constitution. Legislators' words flow like running water and their tempers burn like flaming fire, so they can leap at anything at any time. Occasionally summoned to the court, their words from wheelchairs are not self-deprecation but a display of humility. And they consume this virtue as if it is a chunky rice cake.[31] Neutrality, denoting fairness, transforms into polysemy open to interpretation, and intentional crimes become mere "accidents." As such, the "jarred" world becomes a "jar" that contains everything in the world. Neither Party A nor Party B can escape the clutch-jar of the elderly. How can we simply call these words "play of signifiers?" Ideas (ἰδέα), riding the back of the distorted signifiers and transforming themselves, reveal their nature as ideologies.

4. "This Poem Saved You"

However, this language is not just aggressive. While wordplay surely is a valid strategy for parody, Oh Eun's wordplay goes beyond this. It holds tender confessions, joyous picnics, the honey's flavor that must materialize because it is in the future ("Foreword"), and finally, a beauty that will be attained in due course.

> This poem saved you
> This sentence saved this poem
> This word saved this sentence

31 In Korean, virtue (*deok*) and rice cake (*ddeok*) sound alike.

You saved this word
From the depths of water
You lifted up the word, a soul.

You and the word live in symbiosis
Demanding because they are undemanding
Magnificent because they are trivial

Such are beautiful revolutions

Until you revolve
Somewhere on Earth
Until you rove around, spin around, and finally hang around

Until this word
Becomes the language of the otherworld
Until it is yours and yours only

Until you complete this poem
You are beautiful through and through

—"Salvation"

Salvation is not elsewhere; it resides right here, within these words, sentences, and this poem. In other words, it dwells within the signifier, expression, and the function of language itself. When you pluck a word from the subconscious *sumyeon* ("*sumyeon*" denotes both the surface and sleep), that very word saves you. Why? You and words exist in symbiosis, yet this symbiosis revolves without hitting each other. You cannot encapsulate your entirety in language (what you intend to convey cannot be conveyed), and language can approach you only through deduction (your contours emerge only when surplus is subtracted by the chisel of language). Yet, this revolution envelops us. You and language "rove around, spin around, and finally hang around." That is to say, language hits the target by not hitting the target (the presumption that language hits the target is, after all, a presumption about the language of the hidden). "This word" is always "the language of the otherworld" or the language of an alien land. This signifies that this language, rather than being eroded by universality or ideology, is "yours and only yours." Therefore, a poem like this will never reach completion. If "until you complete this poem / you are beautiful through and through," then you will remain forever beautiful.

Indeed, this would be the case. Because words follow the grammar of signifiers, they are not deciphered in accordance with the signified. Let's expound on the features of these words—namely, the characteristics of dark language. "The fonts attached to a book leaf scamper away, putting on punctuation marks. My favorite word evaporated." ("Dizzying"). Upon adding periods, letters thought they were shoes and ran away in them.[32] Thus, ① languages are already material. Symbols are not intangible signs but embody a material nature. For example, in "it was filled to the brim / all particles / turned toward 'to the brim'" ("Form"), the first "to the brim" (*ggwak*) is an adverb denoting complete fullness. On the other hand, the second "to the brim" has transformed into a box (*gwak*). And this rectangular "*ggwak*" will embody languages.

---

32 In Korean, "punctuation marks" and shoes are homonyms (구두, gudu)

Language naturally encapsulates the world through segmentation, a phenomenon true for both the grammars of the signified and the signifiers. In the grammar of the signified, segmentation is a meaningless notation. In this meaningless segmentation, a specter called "meaning" descends upon it. In the grammar of the signifiers, segmentation is the division of objects, separating and gathering existing entities. In short, ② the segmentation of symbols not only represents the world but also gives birth to the world.

> was I
> beautiful

—Excerpt of "Too Much"

Regrettably, I can only provide an excerpt of this poem like this. Please refer to the full text of the poem in this book. On that page, you will see that the title has evolved into an independent stanza. This disjunction or fusion guides us to two distinct worlds. "too much was I beautiful" is one, and "was I beautiful" is the other. These two statements intricately interact with each other, exchanging "you," "I," "a tree," and "too much" (If you are an astute reader, you would have noticed "nothing" (*mu*) hovering above all these statements).[33] Eventually, they reach the final declaration: "Too much / was I, were you beautiful." This is a beautiful interchange or disorientation between "too much" (*neomunado*) and "tree, you too" (*namu neodo*).

---

33 In Korean, "you," "I," "tree," and "too much" are "neo," "na," "namu," and "neomu," respectively.

If language indeed possesses materiality, it might be possible to describe a person through the combination of sentences. "*Anyone can become great* It becomes possible when a pronoun and a particle unite" ("People who Become Kind Only at Night"). Conversely, dismantling this combination can also break a person's mind. "It becomes enigmatic when a pronoun and a particle unite." In short, the rules of language formation, that is, ③ grammar, are also the principles of life.

> for this room already has many letters
> for hardly anything exists
> literally
> for regularities are rigid
> and irregularities ripple
> when an unexpected sentence crops up
> wriggling through the rift
>
> this room becomes marginally beautiful
> this room becomes marginally distinctive
> this room verges on an alien land
> at last

—Excerpt of "Grammar"

Note that this room (*i bang*) is "an alien land" (*ibang*), identical to "this word" from the earlier poem, "Salvation." While this room harbors numerous letters, there is scarcely anything that "exists / literally." This type of language exists as a special exception, such as an exclamation "Ah," where a single word constitutes a sentence. So, how does language exist? It exists through grammar, i.e., special operational rules that establish lower-order rules and avoid irregularities amid both regularity and irregularity. As language possesses materiality, the operational rules of language—grammar—are also the operational rules of life.

Thus, language and life, more specifically, poetry and life, converge into one. As "Salvation" suggests, acquiring a poem saves a life. This underscores that ④ the world is already one book.

> When I woke up it was morning
> sunlight streamed in
> a breeze drifted and
> a book I hadn't finished rested serenely beside me
>
> If I
> hadn't read this book last night
>
> —Excerpt of "The Medicine Called 'If'"

"The Medicine Called 'If'" is permeated with conditional statements. Starting with "If I had woken up early this morning / If I hadn't missed the subway" and ending with "If I were a better person," these seventeen statements, through conditionals, suggest the realities of different times and spaces not originally given to us. Here, assumptions are not fabrications but rather actualities in alternate dimensions. Within this twisted space-time, language is contorted and returns to square one. In other words, we are provided with a new space-time where the assumption, "If I had woken up early this morning," is materialized. This leads to a sentence like "When I woke up it was morning." Those who failed to wake up and those who overslept on their stomachs are "a book I hadn't finished." Therefore, the subject developing these assumptions is either a book or I, inseparable from a book. If this dream-like subject is indistinguishable from a book, then, by extension, a book is indistinguishable from the world. Hence, the last sentence is written again: "If I / hadn't read this book last night." I am inseparable from a book, and a book is inseparable from the world. Ultimately, I am linked to the world through the clan village of language, embodied in the form of a book. This also attests to the poet's unwavering faith in language.

5. Do You Love Oh Eun?

This is something I actually experienced. I introduced Oh Eun's wordplay during a creative writing class. The next day, a student wrote in their self-introduction that they wanted to attend a university called "Girls' Generation" and didn't want to go to a university called "Blue House" (the Korean presidential residence).[34] Is this the joy that hitches a ride on rhymes, or wordplay that should be condemned? Can we ride this excitement to reach a revolution? Or would we end up immersing ourselves in the denouement of a decadent parody? Whichever it may be, reading Oh Eun's poetry is just like opening a lunchbox on a picnic and seeing it explode. The picnic spot would turn into havoc. The response to this poet sharply divides between the two: embracing playfulness as

34 All three words end in "-dae."—translator

joy and perceiving it as destruction. There is little to no middle ground. Therefore, asking "Do you love Oh Eun?" or "Do you love Oh Eun's poetry?" is also a question about what choices we will make at a crucial point in Korean poetry. I shall respond to this question by transcribing the following poem.

when you open a body, illness
when you open a mouth, a lie
when you open a window, a thief—a thieving cat pops out

when you open a mailbox, an eyeball
when you open tomorrow, a mirage
when you open a door, a tiger—a paper tiger pops out

duplicity is
what the outside with an empty inside does

—"Burst"

How can we ignore the delightful anatomical chart, shepherd boy, and thieving cat? How can we not love the eccentric gaze, illusion, and paper tiger? Whenever time permits, I want to leisurely roll over the intricate fields of this world, tangled with grass and mugwort.

ABOUT THE AUTHOR

Oh Eun received a Bachelor's degree in sociology at Seoul National University and received a Master's degree from the Graduate School of Culture Technology at Korea Advanced Institute of Science and Technology. Oh Eun's poetry collections in Korean include *Pigs at the Hôtel Tassel*, *We Love Atmosphere*, *From Being to Being*, *The Left Hand is Heartbroken*, and *I Had a Name*, as well as essay collections *You Are a Dangerous Robot Right Now*, *You and Me and Yellow*, and *Consolation*. He has won the Park In-hwan Literary Award, the Ku Sang Poetry Award, the Contemporary Poetry Prize, and the Daesan Literature Award. Currently, he is a member of the literary circle Jak-ran.

ABOUT THE TRANSLATOR

Shyun (Suhyun) Ahn 안수현 translates Korean poems to English. He is the translator of Kim Hyun's *Glory Hole*, and he founded and served as the editor-in-chief of *Nabillera: Contemporary Korean Literature*. He graduated from Tufts University with a bachelor's degree in philosophy and international literary and visual studies. After conducting research in East Asian philosophy for four years as a Ph.D. student, he voluntarily left Princeton University's Department of East Asian Studies to join the U.S. Army. Currently, he is a second lieutenant in the Air Defense Artillery.

ABOUT THE SERIES

The Moon Country Korean Poetry Series publishes new English translations of contemporary Korean poetry by both mid-career and up-and-coming poets who debuted after the IMF crisis. By introducing work which comes out of our shared milieu, this series not only aims to widen the field of contemporary Korean poetry available in English translation, but also to challenge orientalist, neo-colonial, and national literature discourses. Our hope is that readers will inhabit these books as bodies of experience rather than view them as objects of knowledge, that they will allow themselves to be altered by them, and emerge from the page with eyes that seem to see "a world that belongs to another star."